A SOCIAL MEDIA SURVIVAL GUIDE

A SOCIAL MEDIA SURVIVAL GUIDE

HOW TO USE THE MOST POPULAR PLATFORMS AND PROTECT YOUR PRIVACY

Melody Karle

ROWMAN & LITTLEFIELD
Lanham • Boulder • New York • London

Published by Rowman & Littlefield
An imprint of The Rowman & Littlefield Publishing Group, Inc.
4501 Forbes Boulevard, Suite 200, Lanham, Maryland 20706
www.rowman.com

6 Tinworth Street, London, SE11 5AL, United Kingdom

British Library Cataloguing in Publication Information Available

Library of Congress Cataloging-in-Publication Data

Names: Karle, Melody A., 1979– author.
Title: A social media survival guide : how to use the most popular platforms and
    protect your privacy / Melody Karle.
Description: Lanham : Rowman & Littlefield, [2020] | Includes bibliographic
    references and index. | Summary: "This book helps those who want to use social
    media but are not necessarily Web-savvy navigate the most popular networking
    sites available. Privacy and technical information about how social media platforms
    function are explained, so everyone can make informed decisions about how to
    connect online."—Provided by publisher.
Identifiers: LCCN 2019038992 (print) | LCCN 2019038993 (ebook) | ISBN
    9781538126790 (cloth) | ISBN 9781538126806 (epub)
Subjects: LCSH: Social media—Handbooks, manuals, etc. | Online social networks—
    Handbooks, manuals, etc.
Classification: LCC HM742 .K375 2020 (print) | LCC HM742 (ebook) | DDC
    302.30285—dc23
LC record available at https://lccn.loc.gov/2019038992
LC ebook record available at https://lccn.loc.gov/2019038993

♾™ The paper used in this publication meets the minimum requirements of
American National Standard for Information Sciences—Permanence of Paper
for Printed Library Materials, ANSI/NISO Z39.48-1992.

CONTENTS

PREFACE

If you have picked up this book, you likely have at least one social media account. You certainly aren't alone: more than 2.77 billion people are using social media in 2019.[1] People all over the world use social media to keep in touch, share news and images, and promote ideas. Even if you do not have a Facebook or Snapchat account, most internet users are exposed to social media networks on a regular basis without even logging in. It is hard to avoid watching YouTube videos that appear in search results, for example. The nightly news and morning talk shows also quote Twitter users, both famous and local. If you are feeling like you don't know enough about the world of social media, this book can help.

This book is intended to help people at all stages of social media discovery. Whether you are already using social media and want to understand it better, or you are trying to decide whether you will enjoy using a certain social media platform, this book breaks down the basics you need to know. Existing social media users are likely to find details about networks that may surprise them. In these pages, you will learn why people choose one platform over another. You will also learn about the terminology used on each platform, as well as the risks and security issues. Overall, *A Social Media Survival Guide* will help everyday people to figure out how to create and manage their social media experience.

A Social Media Survival Guide is not a guide for businesses or people trying to manage the social media presence of a group or company. There are hundreds of books on that topic, and yet remarkably few for the individual person. Rather than telling you how to sell a product, become an influencer, or build a brand, this book will help you learn how to connect with friends, follow news and events, and find information on your chosen platform. It is for regular users who just want to understand how things work. For that reason, things are explained at a basic level. No previous knowledge of each platform is assumed, and the book offers step-by-step explanations with pictures.

Chapter 1, *Social Media Basics*, will provide a foundation for the rest of the book. What is social media? Why do people use it? And *how* do they use it? This chapter demystifies some of the basic ideas behind our use of these amazing (and sometimes infuriating and confusing) technological tools. Chapter 1 also looks at some basic privacy and safety concerns; these also will be explained further in each network-specific chapter.

Chapters 2 through 10 will investigate the most popular social media platforms used most by users in the United States: Facebook, Twitter, YouTube, Snapchat, Instagram, Reddit, LinkedIn, Tumblr, and Pinterest. Each chapter has similar sections so that you can compare different platforms and decide what might work for you. The sections include why people use the platform; terminology; instructions for getting started, creating an account, and using the network; and privacy and safety concerns specific to that platform.

Chapter 11 covers a variety of other notable social media platforms, including dating networks, genealogy networks, messaging apps, and more. Because there are hundreds of social media networks, it is not possible to cover them all in detail. This chapter gives a glimpse into what kinds of niche and special interest platforms exist. Just like the larger chapters, sections in chapter 11 offer explanations, terminology, and privacy tips.

Chapter 12, "Archiving, Saving, and Legacy Management," explains reasoning and issues related to preserving posts and other aspects of social media. Since many people spend a lot of time on social media, saving posts for the future might preserve memories we would otherwise lose. This chapter looks at the different ways someone can save social media posts and information, including built-in and basic tools, as well as special options.

Whether you are looking to build a LinkedIn account to help you look for a job, or want to waste time browsing the Reddit joke feed, this book can help you get started. Read chapter 1 to give you some basic details and foundation. Then, skip around to the platform-specific chapter you need. Make sure to read the chapters for social media platforms you already use, too—you will hopefully learn something new that will improve your experience.

SOCIAL MEDIA BASICS

Social media is part of modern life whether we like it or not. Even if you avoid it in your personal life or limit your time spent on social media, social media comes up a lot. Friends and family post photos and invitations through social media instead of sending e-mails. Our community organizations and churches post to social media instead of sending newsletters or mail announcements as they once did. Television news often shares posts from social media while reporting on everything from the weather to international relations, some from celebrities and political figures but also many from everyday people. In many cases, it is harder to know what is going on without being involved in social media in some way. At the same time, people on social media complain of feeling overwhelmed by their time spent using it. There are also new platforms and applications or "apps" all the time, and data breaches are common. What is the best way to approach your personal use of social media safely, and without burning out (or burning your computer to the ground)? This guide will help you navigate those challenges to become a conscious and thoughtful user of social media.

SO, WHAT IS SOCIAL MEDIA?

Social media is a term used to describe websites and applications designed to facilitate social interaction and content sharing. Some of the most popular platforms include Facebook, Twitter, and YouTube. Social media participants can usually "post" or share comments, images, videos, or audio online through a social media platform. In addition, participants often have a personalized digital space. Sometimes called a user profile, this space is where they can share details about themselves or personalize what others see. Many social media networks also allow users to "follow" one another or otherwise link to another person's account. This allows users to create interactive communities and keep up with content from the people and groups they want to know about.

There are two primary types of social media: social media platforms and messaging applications. Messaging apps include WhatsApp, WeChat, and Viber. These apps are primarily for person-to-person or small-group communications through direct text messages, so they are more conversational than most social media. The difference between messaging and full-featured social media platforms can be confusing because many social media platforms, including Facebook, also have a messaging app. The primary differences between social media platforms and messaging applications is the audience and how individual profiles are used. Messaging applications usually have a focused or targeted audience. Users can choose exactly who is involved in their messages, whether it is one person or a group. While you can include people on a message app that you do not know well, usually these apps are used by friends and groups to share personal communication like a group chat or call. While they can sometimes limit the audience on larger platforms like Instagram, the main use of the larger platforms is to post to a much larger audience. It is also more possible for posts intended for a limited audience to later become viewable by others, since the sharing settings on some platforms change over time.

Most of this book pertains to the larger, full-featured social media platforms. However, many of the issues will also apply to messaging apps and online communication in general. Beyond messaging and social media, suggestions here can also help internet users who post online to a public forum, make comments on a website or blog, or even use e-mail. All of these online communication options could also be called social media if it is defined broadly.

WHY AND HOW DO PEOPLE USE SOCIAL MEDIA?

Social media use is personal and diverse. Everyone may use a certain social media network for different reasons. People looking for a job or to advance their career may use LinkedIn to find opportunities, while those who are not looking for a job might still use LinkedIn for professional networking. Family members may use Instagram to share family photos in a private account. Professional photographers may use Instagram for promoting their work to a large public audience of fans. Each person will find that some social media platforms appeal to them more than others, and they may use them differently than their friends and relatives. And that is okay! There is no one right way to use social media. Even the companies who create social media cannot always anticipate how their product will be used.

Connecting Online and Offline

Social media allows people to connect online and offline. Using photo-sharing websites and social media sites is often an effort for family and friends who know each other in real life to connect more. Sharing photos is easy on most social media and it is much quicker to share a new photo with a large audience online than to send it individually to each person. The same is true of personal news, like a new job, new baby, or engagement. Like a Christmas newsletter that is made to be mailed out to a big group of friends and family, social media can help people give everyone in their online group an update on what has been going on in their lives. The audience also does not have to be family and friends. Reddit users might have a conversation about anything and everything, from local politics to the best pizza, though the participants may never know one another in real life.

Connecting online can also lead to more connection offline. Some social media platforms have event planning tools or make it easy to plan and promote events. Many nonprofits, churches, and community groups use social media to promote their events and organize volunteers. Some social media networks, including Meetup.com and most dating sites, are designed to help people meet in person after connecting first online. While some people will never meet someone in person who they meet online, the possibilities for engaging existing friends as well as building a new community exist on social media platforms.

To Reach an Audience

Another common reason for using social media is to reach an audience. That audience may be a set group of individuals approved individually by the account holder, or it may be the entire world. Social media can be quite public, quite private, and everything in between. People who want to share their thoughts or other creations—be it artistic or just fun—may want to post them online to get feedback and responses. Some platforms, like Twitter, are built to facilitate posts that will reach anyone who looks for them. Even Twitter, though, has an option for a private account, where users can just post to an audience they approved. Most platforms have options that can limit the audience for posted content. Some platforms allow users to choose which posts are public and which are private, so the account holder can choose the audience.

When deciding whether to use a social media platform, users should consider what audience they want to reach. Do they want to post to a large, public forum? If they are making how-to videos that they are hoping others around the world will use, that might make sense. Or are they joining because their family and close friends want them to share baby photos? If so, then posting them publicly may be a privacy risk and probably doesn't make sense. Deciding the desired audience and platform for what you plan to post is important. Whether the intention of joining social media is professional or personal, choose a platform that lets you reach that audience in the best way possible.

To Create, Learn, and Share

Platforms like Flickr, Ravelry, and Pinterest help users create, learn, and share content easily. Often users who interact on these platforms don't know each other in real life but connect virtually because of a shared interest. Ravelry.com, a network for people who knit and crochet, lets users share patterns, photos, and information about their shared love of yarn crafting. Pinterest lets users create digital bulletin boards where they can save images they like or want to use for a project, such as ideas for a new home they want to build. These and similar platforms can be helpful tools for people's creative and educational endeavors online.

Creative platforms can be very social or barely social; you can watch a YouTube video without commenting or liking, and you can view patterns on Ravelry without engaging other users. However, social aspects exist on the platforms that make it easy for people to connect when they want to. Pinterest boards for a wedding can easily be shared with the bridal party, for example. As with many aspects of social media, what users choose to share depends on the platform, the chosen audience, and the privacy controls available.

Staying Informed/News

While many social media networks were intended to be places where individual people interacted on a personal level, social media sites are also great for keeping up with news and events. Sites like Reddit and Nextdoor can keep users up to date on what is going on at their college, town, or other community. People can ask questions semi-anonymously and find out information from people who live nearby or across the world. All major news outlets, and even most small newspapers and television and radio stations, have social media accounts where they post the latest articles or information. Sometimes a news Twitter feed posts information long before a full story is available. Many users also enjoy the ability to tailor their news sources and reach them all in the same spot. For example, a Twitter user can choose to follow all of the people in their professional field, all of their favorite sports teams, and their favorite local and national news sources so that they receive a feed of specific things they want to see.

City governments, police and emergency responders, and elected officials all use social media to keep people informed. In emergency situations, like floods and other natural disasters, social media is sometimes the most reliable way to find out the very latest information. Facebook and some other networks have a check-in feature, which lets users in an area affected by a disaster check in as "safe" so that loved ones know their status. Emergency response teams may use social media to post the latest news, whereas updating their website is sometimes slower and not as easy to do.

Social media can also be used to keep up with churches, community groups, and nonprofits. Social platforms are popular with these groups because most platforms are free and help them engage their supporters easily. People who feel overwhelmed by e-mails from too many groups may prefer to follow them on a social media platform, where they can check things as they are able rather than having e-mails pile up in an inbox. Further, some people *only* follow groups or news entities on their chosen platform (rather than "real" people, like friends and family). In this way, a social media user can use a specific platform as a news-only feed, without baby and kitten pictures getting in the way.

Observing Is Okay

As previously stated, everyone uses social media in a different way, and "lurking" is just as valid a use of social media as anything else. *Lurking* is a term used to describe people who are on social media but rarely post or contribute. Lurking is not the same as being inactive. Inactive participants create an account but rarely log in or look at the site at all—they are not participating because they are not there. Lurkers, who might also be called observers, are there to see the updates, watch the videos, read the posts, and keep up with all of the other things people do—except react. And that is okay! Private people and people who consider themselves introverts may find this approach appealing because they do not like to publicly post their opinions online. If you want to have a Twitter account and never tweet a thing, that is just fine. And the same goes for Facebook, Instagram, and most other platforms. Where this might not make sense is on professional platforms like LinkedIn. If you join a professional network, you probably do want to create at least a basic professional profile—but more about that in chapter 8.

PRIVACY AND SAFETY BASICS

A major concern about using the internet in general—and social media specifically—is privacy and safety. Each platform has its own risks and issues, as will be discussed in later chapters. However, there are some basics that can apply to all platforms. It is impossible to say that any online activity is totally safe and secure, but that should not stop people from using the tools online, including social media. Just like driving, which also has risks, users should be cautious and aware of their surroundings while they are online. Yes, it is always possible that a system could get hacked, and there is sometimes nothing that can be done. In many cases, though, there are ways to reduce the risks.

What Gets Posted Online Stays Online Forever—True?

Librarians and high school teachers like to tell students that they need to be careful of what they text to others or post online because it will live online forever. But is that true? Well, yes and no. The sad thing is that many important things are posted and later lost without an option to retrieve them. That is why it is important to back up personal files; no one else cares as much about photos of your grad school thesis or high school graduation as you do (maybe your parents). The issue is that people on the internet—the general audience of your own relations and random strangers—don't usually share things like that. People tend to share things that are funny, embarrassing, incriminating, and awful. Those are the things that are likely to have a long or even eternal life on the internet because multiple people see them, share them, and save them. Yes, it is possible that anything you share digitally may end up staying online for a long time. The safest thing is to think of anything you post online as being public. Be especially careful of sensitive or personal photos, videos, and comments.

Be Wary of Other Users

Social media users should always be wary of other people's intentions online, no matter how good natured they may seem. Many privacy risks come from people we think we know, or even people we do know if an account has been hacked. If a person you know tries to contact you online, but something seems "off" about the language they use, or they are asking for something unusual, check with the person by another means (like text or e-mail). It is possible their account has been hacked and someone is trying to get private information from you. Depending on the platform, it may make sense to only connect with people you know well, especially if you post personal details often. It is okay to not respond to connection requests if you don't know someone or don't want to be connected online. Nowadays, many people limit some social media use to family only, and people usually understand.

Online dating and meetup sites can be wonderful, but users need to be smart about the personal information they share with people they don't know yet. A lot of the personal information people share on dating sites is similar to security questions and answers used for online banking: things like the names of pets, hometown, and favorite foods. It can be sad to think of people using dating sites to scam other people. We all want to think the best of people. But this sort of scam does happen. If you get a bad feeling about someone you can cut off the conversation at any time. When and if you do meet people in person who you first met online, always meet in a public place and let other people know when and where the meeting is happening.

Everyone on social media should also be aware of a behavior called trolling. *Trolling* is an internet slang term for when people online try to bait others into having a reaction to their posts and comments. These people are trolling others (usually random people they do not know) by posting offensive comments and picking fights to get a reaction. It is not clear what trolls get out of this experience other than knowing they can get other people worked up. Users who are aware of this sort of behavior can recognize it for what it is and walk away from an online argument rather than engaging a troll online.

Choose Connections Consciously

Oddly, there is a lot of social pressure to be connected online. Users who have findable accounts may get requests from coworkers, neighbors, and other people they just don't know that well. It is okay to say no or not respond to requests. Some platforms allow you to hide your account so that it is more difficult to find unless someone knows your screen name or handle. Where possible, limit connections by making your accounts harder to find with available settings. If that isn't what you want, you can also usually limit what you see from people you don't know well. Just don't forget that they are there! Having 500 connections may feel great but it is easy to forget who is there when you post something.

There are things that may be appropriate for your aunt but not your college friends, or your neighbor but not your boss. For nonpublic and nonprofessional accounts, it does not hurt to review your social media connections periodically and remove connections to people you may never see again.

Review Privacy Settings

It should go without saying, but every social media user should review the available account settings on the platforms they are using. Users should do this when they sign up for a new account and then should watch for any updates and changes from the platform. Usually the social media site will e-mail changes to the user agreement or new security features. Even if there is no update, it is helpful to review settings on accounts you use often. Many of the settings may not be helpful to every user, but it is good to know what is there and what is not. Can you set posts or an entire account as private or limit to certain groups? Can people find your account with a Google search? Can they search for you directly if they have your e-mail address? Also, be aware of how to report abuse if it happens. For example, if someone were to make threatening comments, how would that be reported? Can you block people? Know what is okay to post and not post on that specific platform so you are following the rules, too. And yes, you really should update your password often. This is especially true if there are news reports of a possible data breach on a social media platform you use. More on specific platform privacy settings is covered in later chapters.

Know How to Safely Share Photos

You might notice the convenience of cell phone and computer programs "knowing" where photographs were taken: your phone can organize all your vacation photos for you, and your Instagram account suggests a location tag to add—because it knows where you took the photo. This happens because your camera phone attaches location data to the image. This data is usually specific enough to find the exact address. If you think about it, there are many reasons why you would not want specific location details attached to photos you share. For example, if you have a photo of your daughter that was taken at your home and you post it to your Facebook or Flickr account, do you know whether someone can download the photo and find the geographic coordinates to your house? The short answer is usually no, but it isn't that simple.

Many of the "big" social media platforms, including Facebook, do strip out a lot of that data. But others, especially new and smaller sites, may not. Location features on Twitter and Flickr can be turned off. However, online file sharing sites like Google Drive and Dropbox do not strip any data at all, so being privacy savvy is important if you use many online sharing sites. Facebook and Instagram do strip out location data, though, as well as reducing file quality. And that is both good *and* bad. While it protects your privacy in some ways, it also erases that data for anyone with whom you legitimately want to share photos. If you post a photo to Facebook and your mom drags it to her desktop, she will not get any of those location data, like she would if you had e-mailed her the photo. Plus, the photo is usually reduced in size, so it might not look good if she tries to have prints made. You also cannot expect to store all of your photos on Facebook, download them later, and still have high-quality images that your photo management software can tag for you.

So, what does this mean? Yes, it is safe to share online, but do it thoughtfully. Don't post photos to any platform with full geographic information without thinking about it first and checking to see if geographic information is included. Share things on Facebook that you want people to see, but send your mom the better-quality photos on a flash drive or through Dropbox. Most important, for safety, don't text, e-mail, or share photos on file-sharing sites to people you don't know well, unless they were taken somewhere public that you don't mind them knowing.

Maintain Your Profile, Account, and Posts

If you have a personal profile, revisit it occasionally to make sure you like what it says. It is easy to forget what you put there a year ago, and it may no longer represent what you want it to say about you. This is particularly true if you are using a public platform, where random strangers may come across your posts or profile. Depending on the kind of network and how much information you add to your profile, you may also want to update account information like phone number and backup e-mail address, which is sometimes used to unlock your account if there is a problem. On a professional website like LinkedIn, make sure your job title and responsibilities are kept accurate, especially if you are up for promotion or looking for a raise. Individual posts can also be weeded. If you scroll through old posts and find that something there no longer makes sense, or you would prefer that it is no longer on your page, you can usually delete it. Keep in mind, it may still be hanging around out there somewhere—more on that later.

Things Never to Post on Social Media

- Photos of yourself at home, unless you know how to remove the embedded location in the photographs, or you know the platform removes it for you.
- Naked or sexual photos of yourself or anyone else. This is not only dangerous but also is against the user agreement rules for most social media accounts.
- Travel plans, especially if you live alone. This can invite break-ins while you are away.
- Home address and phone number. If people are your friends, they likely already know this information. If they don't, send them a direct message rather than posting this information to a large audience.
- Financial status or information, such as how much you make, photos of cash or valuables, or implications that you are a good target for theft or scams.

Tips and Cautions/Best Practices for All Platforms

- Log out periodically on all devices. This is just good practice. It can help you remember your password (unless you have it saved), and it also prevents people from hacking your account. Accounts that are always logged in make it easier for online hackers to get in and get your information.
- Search for yourself from a computer or phone you don't own, or from someone else's account (ask first!). This includes a basic Google search, as well as searches on the social media platforms you use. This will help you understand what other people see when they are looking at your online profiles. It may be surprising to see how much is available publicly and even how much appears to friends.
- Assume a lack of privacy. Most platforms let you limit your audience, yes, but that audience may treat your information differently than you intended. Snapchat, for example, has made a name for itself by making messages non-savable. Some users get around this by taking a photo of their phone with another device. If someone wants to share or save something, they will find a way, so it is best to avoid sending sensitive things on any digital platform.
- Adjust privacy and personal settings when you sign up, and then periodically review them in case things have changed. Quick tip: they change often.

- Don't log in to other platforms and accounts using Facebook or other social media platform logins. Some accounts let you use your Facebook or Google account to log in to another account. This puts you at greater risk if your account is compromised because it gives access to more than just the hacked account.
- Don't add financial accounts to your social media page. Yes, it can make it easier to buy things that are advertised on the pages, or to donate to a good cause. It also makes you vulnerable to security breaches. You can still buy things through social media accounts if you want, but do it safely: though it takes slightly longer, add your credit card number each time instead of saving it in your account.
- Delete unused/dead accounts. It is usually harmless to keep older accounts open even if you are not using them, but it isn't good practice. People may continue to find you and try to make contact with no response. Also, it is easy to forget what you posted there until it comes up much later, perhaps when you no longer have the e-mail address associated with the account. Then it is basically there forever. Not ideal!
- Don't save passwords unless the device you are using is password protected. In other words, don't save the login to all of your accounts on your phone, then not keep your phone locked and password protected. Even then, be cautious allowing your device to retain passwords, especially on mobile devices. While password saving is common and allows for quick use of your social media account, it can also make it easy for someone to hack your account.
- Change your password often, and don't use passwords that can be figured out by looking at your social media page. That means pet names, nicknames, and street names should be out of the running for password use.

GETTING THE MOST OUT OF EACH PLATFORM

Internet users can get the most out of social media platforms by being informed and thinking about how they want to participate. Decide why you are there, and then act the part. If you are on a general social media page where you are keeping up with friends and family, then perhaps anything goes. But if you are on a site to share your artwork and say as much on your profile, then it is confusing to people who follow you if you also decide to post a long list of complaints about your local city government. Ravelry isn't the right place to get in a fight about politics, but Twitter and Reddit might work if that is what you are looking for.

Once you decide what social media platforms appeal to you, decide if you have specific goals for your time there. If you just want an outlet for your thoughts, that is okay. If your goals are more specific or professional, save your personal thoughts for a different account or platform.

Just because you have an account doesn't mean you need the app. Being online constantly can be stressful, and having a constant ping or alert from your phone can add to you feeling overwhelmed by social media. If the constant contact is more stressful than enjoyable, consider whether you want or need the app on your phone. Almost all social media sites are available from a desktop computer, and limiting time on a site might be as easy as saying "I will only check it from home." Whether that means only having an app on a tablet or desktop at home, or turning off the notifications, users should remember to set notifications and decide how they will interact with a platform to fit their lives.

FACEBOOK

With more than 61 million American users, Facebook continues to be the most popular social media platform in the United States.[1] Even if you have managed not to have a Facebook account, it is very unlikely that you have not heard of Facebook. Facebook has been in the public spotlight many times, with news articles about privacy concerns, fake news, and even the company's plans to bring free internet to the world's poorest countries.[2] If you already have an account, there are probably some things about Facebook you do not know: controls and features change all the time.

WHY DO PEOPLE USE FACEBOOK?

The most common reason people use Facebook is to stay in touch with other people. People share life events, including new baby photos, marriage announcements, relocations, and other big news, as well as smaller updates about life. As with many social media outlets, posts from people you do not talk with often can help you stay up to date on what is happening in their lives. Since Facebook is the largest platform, it is likely that many of the people you know use it. This not only includes your friends but also your coworkers and extended family.

Of all the social media platforms in America, Facebook is the most popular. Facebook is the most widely used social media platform by American adults, but it is becoming less popular with younger generations.[3] This is in part because there are so many new social media platforms. However, it can be difficult to close an account if you are already using Facebook, even if you like another network better. Not everyone has started using other social media, and those who have are all using different platforms from one another. Facebook still has the largest network. Disconnecting from Facebook means disconnecting from those friends and family members you do not see or hear from often. Businesses and schools also advertise events on the site, and organizations and churches use Facebook for outreach. Many charities post their news on their account pages, requiring users to occasionally log in if they want to stay in the loop. Some businesses do not even have a separate website and instead use Facebook as the primary place to share content online, including restaurant menus, announcements, and location details like hours. Some of these details are viewable without a Facebook account, but it is hard for some people to avoid Facebook without feeling like they are missing information that is just not available on other platforms.

Facebook has a number of features that help people with projects and organization. Facebook's event planning feature lets people plan public events or private ones like a birthday party. People can say whether they are going to the event, can comment, and can invite other people (if the event planner allows it). Facebook then reminds attendees when the event is happening soon. *Groups* is another feature that helps people organize together. Whether it is a school alumni group, a reading club, a support group, or a team of volunteers, Facebook groups let people who may or may not be Facebook friends communicate and discuss common issues. Facebook even has built-in fundraising capabilities, so you can support your favorite charity right through the site.

Another reason people use Facebook is nostalgia. Facebook has been around so long now that it offers flashbacks to posts and photos from years ago. If you have had an account for a long time, you can look back over your posts and reread the comments others have added. For example, you can look at the birth announcement of your son or daughter and see all of the positive comments from well-wishers. These sorts of responses used to come as cards in the mail, but that rarely happens anymore. Now, Facebook serves as a digital guest book for these sorts of life events. Even if you have not had your account for a long time, you can look back at the history of your friends' posts. Many people have more than a decade of sharing and photos on the site, making it a huge repository of social sharing.

FACEBOOK TERMINOLOGY

Check In—Facebook lets you change your status to "check in" at your current location. You can add a photo or message, but there will also be a map and named location to show your friends where you were. You must allow Facebook location access to use this function (see figure 2.1).

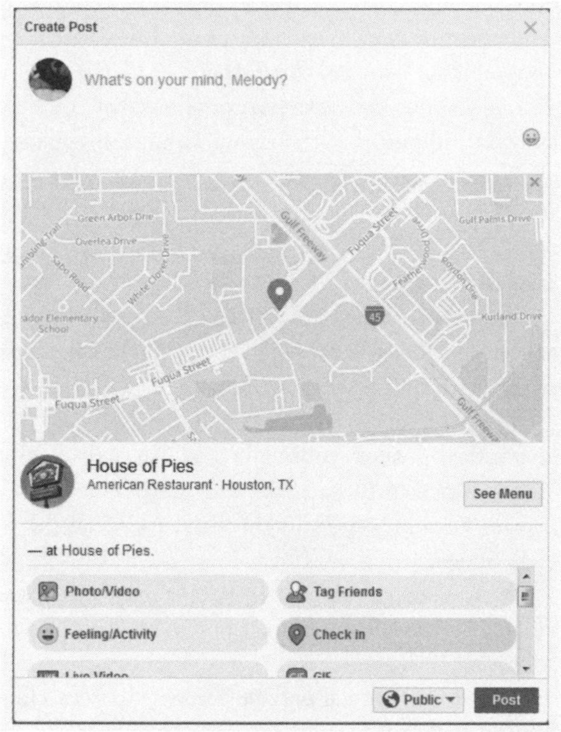

Figure 2.1. Facebook allows you to "check in" at a location.

Follow—Following on Facebook means that you will get updates from that person or group in your news feed. You automatically follow people you are friends with. You can also choose to follow pages for non-people, including churches, businesses, schools, and organizations.

Friends—Being friends on Facebook lets you and another person see each other's posts and accounts. You can search for friends by name on Facebook, or Facebook may suggest people that you might know based on shared friends, school, and workplace. You can become Facebook friends with other people but not with groups or businesses.

Groups—Groups are collections of people on Facebook who may or may not be Facebook friends but have some shared interest. For example, a high school alumni group or an animal rescue volunteer group may create a Facebook group to share news and chat with one another.

Life Event—When you share an important event in your life, such as getting married, moving to a new home, or getting a new job, you can specially mark the event on Facebook as a Life Event. Life Events are usually bigger news than everyday posts, so they will be prioritized in your friends' news feeds so they don't miss the news. You can see your Life Events by going to your profile (click on your name), then clicking About.

Like—When you see a post or photo that you like, you can click on the Like (thumbs up) button to share your feelings. If you mouse over the like button (or click to choose on the mobile app) you can also choose a heart, laughing face, wow face, sad face, or angry face. Facebook created the original like button, and most other social media networks have followed suit with something similar because it is a popular feature.

News Feed / Home—Your news feed is the running list of posts from people and groups that you see when you log in to Facebook. You can always get back to the news feed by clicking Home.

Snooze—You can snooze a person, page, or group to get a 30-day break from seeing their posts in your news feed. No one sees that they have been snoozed, and their news will start showing up again automatically after the 30 days. To snooze someone, click the three-dot menu on the upper right of the post and click Snooze.

Stories—Facebook Stories is a second news feed where users can create video and photo content that they want to share with a specific audience for a short time. Using the Facebook app, you can use built-in filters to enhance photos and video that will only be available to your chosen audience for 24 hours. The functionality is similar to using Snapchat.

Tag—When you create a post or add a photograph on Facebook, you have the option to tag a friend or page on Facebook. This will usually happen automatically when you start to type in a person's name, and you can choose from the list of names that appears. This tag will create a link that other people can click on to see the person's page. Tagging the person will also make the post show up on that person's page (unless they have set their preferences not to).

Verified—Pages or profiles on Facebook that have a check mark next to them have been verified. That means that Facebook has identified them as being authentic: they are who they say they are. This helps you to know whether a news site, page, or public figure is correct.

THE BASICS OF USING FACEBOOK

You can access Facebook through the website on a computer or mobile device, as well as through mobile apps for phones and tablets. To create a new Facebook account, download the Facebook app or go to Facebook.com and enter your name, e-mail address, and/or mobile phone number, password, date of birth, and gender. Facebook policy requires that you use a real or "authentic" name on the platform so that people can clearly identify you as someone they know.[4] This policy has caused problems resulting in people's accounts being removed or suspended. Facebook will also remove individual accounts for animals (for example, if you created a page for your cat). Your birthday is used to identify whether you are old enough to have an account: you must be 13 years old or older to use Facebook. Beyond name and birthday, users can also choose gender as male, female, or custom (custom allows users to type in what they want).

Personal Facebook accounts must also be for individuals, not businesses or groups. For an entity including a cause, celebrity, business, or band, you can create a nonpersonal page. A nonpersonal page works differently than a personal page in several key ways. First, you cannot be friends with a nonpersonal page. Instead, you can follow it to get news and updates. Following a business or group page this way protects your privacy, since the administrators of that page cannot see your page or information unless it is public, even though you follow them. To create a nonpersonal page, go to the link under the login/sign up fields on Facebook.com. If you already have an individual page, you can also create a page for your business or cause. However, Facebook policy prohibits an individual from creating two different individual pages for themselves. While this still happens all the time, Facebook will suspend pages for people who have duplicate accounts if they discover them.

Once you have an account, you can customize your profile in several ways. Click on your name or profile image to go to your profile. Holding your mouse over your cover image (the large image along the top of your profile) or your round profile image will give you the option to change them. You can upload a photo or choose a photo you have already added to Facebook. Facebook will also offer frames (color and images that go around your photo) that you can use based on current events, things that are popular, or what you have expressed interest in. For example, you might see a frame for your favorite *American Idol* choice, or the local Humane Society if you have shown interest in them previously. You can choose the frame permanently or have it automatically turn off after an hour, day, or week (see figure 2.2). Your profile also has places to add lots of information about you: an introduction about yourself, your current city and hometown, where you work, what you do, your schools, and your favorite things. These can be adjusted under the About tab or in the profile sidebar. You can also choose to link your other social media and websites to Facebook and add life events like graduations, kids, and new jobs.

Connecting with friends is a large part of Facebook. Friends will be able to see your profile and your posts and can interact with you through Facebook more than a nonfriend could. Until you are friends, others will not be able to see your posts or account information unless you have set things to public viewing. If you add your schools, workplace, and location, Facebook will recommend friends to you. You can also search for people you know in the main search bar. When you search a name, you will see all search results including people. You can click People to see a full list of people who match that name. If you are not already friends, you can click the Add Friend button to connect with them. They will need to accept your friend request for you to become friends. Similarly, if someone asks you to be friends you will have to agree before your

Figure 2.2.   Frame options allow you to customize your profile image.

accounts are linked. If you add family members and relationships, you can go to About > Family and Relationships to link to people who have specific relationships with you. You can designate someone as your spouse or boyfriend, and you can designate others as your aunt, sister, or father, and so on. Facebook will send the person a confirmation when you link to them in this way, and the status will say *Pending* until they agree.

Managing your friends and knowing who you are friends with is important, since you will be sharing information with them when you post things. Once you have some friends, Facebook will recommend more people to you that are friends of friends. In some cases, you will know those people, but it is okay to ignore Facebook's recommendations, whether or not you know the person. You do not have to connect to everyone you know on Facebook (although some people do). You can also review your friends at any time by going to your profile page (click on your name or profile picture) and selecting Friends. Facebook will show a list of all of your friends; it includes options for seeing those from your current city or those from your hometown. If you have a lot of friends, you can search for them by name using the search bar above the list. You can also control friend settings by clicking on the button next to each friend. Options include turning on or off notifications from that friend, adding the friend to a list (such as close friends or acquaintances), or unfriending them. Adding friends to a certain list is one way to control privacy since Facebook allows you to post or control settings based on specific lists. For example, you could post something and only include people you have marked as close friends. Click on a friend's name to go to their profile page.

You can also create and share posts once your account is set up. Click on Home to go to your main news feed. The open box at the top of the screen marked "Create Post" will usually have a question in it, such as "What's on your mind?" or "What's new?" Click in the box and type in a message about your day, your thoughts, or anything else you want to share. Clicking in the box will make it larger and show more options (see figure 2.3). You can use the options to add media, such as a photo, GIF, or video. You can add a feeling or activity, such as what you are eating or what emotion you are feeling (see figure 2.4). You can also ask for recommendations, add a background, tag an event that you are attending, choose a nonprofit to promote with your post, create a poll, or make a list to share. Using the Check In option will use location services (if you allow it) to find nearby places. To do that, choose the location you are at from the list Facebook provides and virtually "check in" there so that people know where you were when you posted. If you don't allow Facebook to use your location, you can still check in by searching for the place manually. Similarly, you can tag friends in your posts. Finding their names and tagging them in your post usually means they were with you when you posted, but it could also mean they were mentioned or you want them to know about the post. You can also tag them by mentioning them by name in your post: their image and name should appear when you start to type the name. Tagging friends will alert them that they have been tagged so it is harder to miss the post. You can also choose to live stream video by choosing that option from the Post menu.

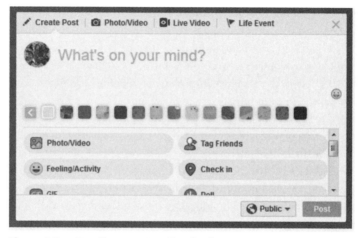

Figure 2.3. Creating a post on Facebook.

Using Facebook to keep up with businesses, causes, and organizations can also be helpful. Many groups use Facebook to create and distribute information about events. You can find nonindividual pages two different ways. First, you can search for a specific business, cause, or organization using the main search bar. You can limit the search results to just pages from the list along the top. A list of pages will appear with a name, type of page (public figure, community, business, website, cause, place, band, etc.). Each result will also show you how many people like and follow the page. By clicking the Like button next to a page name, you will start following that page and will get news from the page in your news feed. Do keep in mind that Facebook algorithms prevent all posts from followed pages from showing up on all pages, so if you want to see the most current news from a page you should navigate directly to it. If you click on the page name you can see the full page, including photos, posts, lists, and more. Nonprofits may have a button that allows you to support them with a donation through the site. Another way to find pages is to click on Pages under Explore, then choose Top Suggestions or Invites (see figure 2.5). Top suggestions will

Figure 2.4. You can add a feeling or emotion to your Facebook post, if desired.

show you pages for things similar to those you have liked through Facebook. Invites will show you pages that Facebook friends have invited you to like.

Friends can share, like, comment, and respond to one another's posts, and anyone on Facebook can respond to posts from pages they like and follow. Whether you see a post directly on a person's page or in your news feed, there are multiple options available for responding to a post. The Like option looks like a thumbs up and is the most basic way to respond if you like the post. The same button offers options for love, haha (laughing face), wow (surprised face), sad (crying face), and angry (red face). You can also comment on the post in the open space below it. Comments can be just text or emoji, pictures, GIFs, or stickers, which are pasted images that you can choose from (see figure 2.6). You may also see a Share option if the post is shareable; not all posts are shareable if the person posting has chosen to limit that option. There are also some options in the upper right of every post in the three-dot menu, including the Give Feedback on This Post option. That is where you can report a post for nudity, violence, harassment, suicide concern, fake news, hate speech, and other issues.

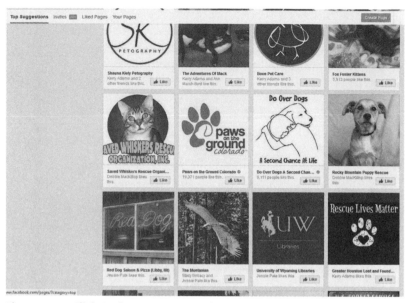

Figure 2.5.   Click Explore to see pages that Facebook suggests for you.

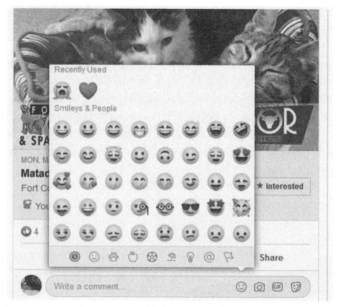

Figure 2.6.   There are multiple options for commenting on a post, including emojis and stickers.

When you log in to Facebook or visit the app, you will see notifications as red numbers that appear for different activity on the site (see figure 2.7). A number over the little people icon means that you have pending friend requests. You can click on the icon to confirm or delete requests. Deleting a request will not notify the person that the request was deleted—they may just think you have not responded yet. Notifications over the speech bubble with the lightning bolt are Messenger notifications. This means that someone has sent you a private chat message. On a mobile device, you will need to have a separate app, Facebook Messenger, to read the chat. However, on a computer you can click on the icon to see the chat in a smaller window. Notifications over the bell icon tell you about important posts, such as posts you are mentioned in or posts where you have been tagged. You can view the post by clicking on it, or you can choose to mark it as read so that it disappears from your notifications. You can control what notifications you see in your settings, which is linked from the top of the Notifications list. You can also access it in your account settings by clicking on the down arrow > Settings.

Figure 2.7.   Facebook notifications.

Settings has a lot of options that help you control and change your preferences. It can be overwhelming to look through all the settings options, but it can make your experience using Facebook more enjoyable. Many of the settings are linked throughout the platform so you can adjust things while you are viewing them. However, the main place to adjust settings all together is by clicking on the down arrow and choosing Settings. Choose from the many options to see lists of possible settings changes, including Privacy, Location, Notifications, Apps and Websites, Timeline and Tagging, and more.

Facebook Events

You can create, search for, and RSVP for events using Facebook's event-planning feature. Facebook may suggest events to you based on your interests or if your friends indicate that they may attend. Friends may also invite you to events they create or are planning to attend. You can choose Events from the sidebar list or use the search bar at the top of the screen to browse or search for events. You can narrow events by location, time period, and type of event (including food, comedy, games, art, and more). If you plan to attend an event, you can click the Going option to add your name to the likely attendee list. Your friends and the event planners will be able to see that you plan to attend. If you aren't sure, you can also choose Maybe, and you can share your regrets by selecting Can't Go. You can also share events or click on the event title to comment or discuss the event with others.

Facebook Messenger

Facebook Messenger is Facebook's private chat feature linked to your Facebook account. It allows two or more people to chat privately, much like they would using SMS or any other messaging app. Messenger chats do not appear to your friends or followers unless they are part of the chat. On a computer, you can use Messenger by clicking on the icon that looks like a speech bubble with a lightning bolt and searching for the person you want to message. Alternatively, you can go to a person's profile page and click on the same icon next to the Message option. A chat screen will appear where you can video or audio chat, post images, post emojis, add stickers, play a game together, or even send money. Using Facebook Messenger on a mobile device requires a second app since you cannot access Messenger chats through the regular Facebook mobile app.

PRIVACY AND SAFETY

Keeping up on Facebook privacy and safety can be challenging. However, the company has been in the spotlight so many times for privacy concerns that they have made them a priority: there are lots of options for controlling your privacy on Facebook. Almost all sections of Facebook (including individual posts, settings, and profile) have options for controlling privacy at a micro or macro level (meaning you can change it for one post or all posts, one friend or all friends, etc.). That can make it hard to remember where everything is located. Get into the habit of checking your settings on a regular basis to see what has changed and to make sure everything is as it should be. You can review account settings by clicking on the down arrow icon and choosing Settings.

It is important to understand the privacy risks of being part of any large network. Like most social media platforms, Facebook is free. It makes its money through advertising. It regularly provides information about Facebook users to potential advertisers, and all Facebook users agree to this in the user agreement when they sign up for Facebook. Additionally, many people become friends with people they do not know well. These may be neighbors, old friends, old coworkers, and even friends of friends. Having hundreds of friends may put you at risk if you share private information. You can control some of what you share by setting some friends as "Close Friends" and only posting more personal posts to that group. You can also set an individual to "restricted," which means they will not see any of your posts unless they are set to public, where anyone can view them whether or not they are your friend. Setting a person to "restricted" will not alert them of their status change. You can make the change by going to your list of friends and clicking on the Friends button > Add to Another List > Restricted. No matter who you post to, though, it is helpful to occasionally review your list of friends and remove anyone that you do not really know.

Facebook asks for more information about you than many other social networks. Much of that information can be kept private from the general public. However, once Facebook has that information the company may use it for many reasons, including targeted advertising. Be conscious of what information you choose to add to your account. You can also choose to add just your e-mail or your mobile phone number—you don't have to add both unless you want to. You can also choose to hide your birthday and can choose a gender different than what appears on your identification. Account settings to review include Privacy, Location, Blocking, Face Recognition, Apps and Websites, and Ads.

Some Safety Tips for Facebook

- You can report a post for nudity, violence, harassment, fake news, hate speech, or other problem or safety issues by clicking on the three-dot menu in the upper right of the post and choosing Give Feedback on This Post.
- Turn off your birthday reminder. Facebook requires a birthday in your account, but you can turn off the option to display your birthday to friends. If you have a small group of friends who already know your birthday, this might not matter. However, if you have many friends who are more casual relations, hiding your birthday can protect you against identity theft. You can also choose to share the day of your birth but not the year, or share the date with only certain groups of friends. To hide your birthday or birth year, click on your name or profile image and click on About. Under Contact and Basic Info, hover your mouse over your birth date or birth year. Click Edit and then the lock icon to change the settings for who can see this information (see figure 2.8).

- Avoid giving other apps or programs access to your Facebook account. This is easier said than done: many fun features and apps from other companies want access in order to make things work. Without them, you cannot use those tools, apps, or fun programs. Whenever you are asked to give account access to an outside app or program, pause to consider whether you feel okay with another company having access to everything Facebook knows about you.
- Related to not providing access to third-party apps, it is also a good idea to review the apps you have already granted access to your account. Erase any that you no longer use or do not recognize. To do this, go to the down-arrow menu > Settings > Apps and Websites and review active apps that have access to your account.
- Many people have had an account on Facebook for years. They may not remember what they posted years ago, but all of it is still visible. Some

Figure 2.8. Hide your birthday or birth year.

of it may actually be more visible based on how privacy terms may have changed on Facebook over the years. Make time to review your account all the way back to the beginning and periodically delete things that you no longer want to be "out there" for everyone to see. You can click the three-dot menu on any of your old posts and hide or delete it.

- You can turn off the ability of others to tag you in photographs. You can also add the option to be notified and approve photos that others want to tag you in. To do this, go to the down-arrow menu > Settings > Timeline and Tagging.
- Facebook does not vet people's identities. If someone wants to start a new Facebook page with your name and photo they can do it, although it violates Facebook's terms of use. If someone reaches out to you claiming to be a long lost friend or family member, general internet rules apply even if the name and photo are familiar: do not send money or give out private account or financial information to anyone online.

SPECIAL FEATURES AND HELP

Facebook Help is very full featured and available from the app or website by clicking on the blue question mark icon. Facebook offers options including Report a Problem, Privacy Checkup, Updating Your Info, and more. You can also ask a question in the help field or follow the link to the Help Center for more information.

Memorials are Facebook pages for those who have passed away. Memorial pages are not created by families: they are the pages that the person had when they were alive, memorialized in accordance with their wishes. People can set another Facebook member as their Legacy Contact. That person can decide what to do with the account if a person passes away. To set your Legacy Contact, go to the down-arrow menu > Settings > General and click on Edit next to Manage Account. You can even set a reminder to review your Legacy Contact once a year.

Your interests are tracked on Facebook using the information you add to your profile. It can be interesting and, honestly, a little weird to review what the site has collected about you—especially if you have been on Facebook for a long time (see figure 2.9). To see what interests Facebook has listed for your account, go to the down-arrow menu > Settings > Ads. You can review your interests and remove some if they are inaccurate (or you just don't want them linked to your account). The ads section also shows you what advertisers have ads using a list that contains information about you. Make sure to also check the information under "Your Information" > "Your Categories" to see things like suspected political party, devices owned, and travel activity.

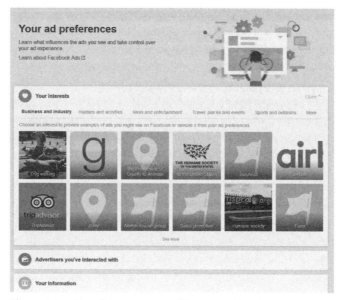

Figure 2.9.   Your interests, according to Facebook.

TWITTER

Twitter is a highly popular social networking platform that allows users to share "tweets" that can include short messages, images, news, and other media. Twitter is widely used by individuals, companies, and government officials. Users create a profile where they can share their own messages, usually publicly, as well as view tweets from others. Twitter users can choose people and organizations to follow, so that they see any updates on their personalized feed. However, unless the account is private (which is uncommon), anyone can search for and find a tweet from anyone, regardless of whether they follow that person or that person follows them. Twitter is one of the most popular social media platforms, with more than 330 million active users per month (see figure 3.1).[1]

WHY DO PEOPLE USE TWITTER?

Because it is primarily a public platform, Twitter attracts people who want a broad audience for their posts, as well as people who want to hear from a large variety of sources. It can also be the best place to find immediate and unfiltered information from a community about something that is happening. For example, Twitter often has more specific location information about the status and safety of an area during news events, natural disasters, and other crises. This is because individuals who are witnessing an event live can share their experiences before mainstream "official" news services arrive and report.

Unlike Facebook, which has no character limit, posts to Twitter are required to be short. This makes it easier to view more news and information quickly.

Figure 3.1.   View of Twitter.

Sometimes tweets will contain a link to a full article or more information, but basic tweets are just short thoughts or comments without additional background. Hypothetically, the character limit requires people to put some thought into their tweets in order to keep them short. In practice, however, Twitter is a mix of well-crafted as well as random and poorly written tweets. Proponents of the platform enjoy the diversity and randomness, but it may not be for everyone.

A common use of Twitter by famous and nonfamous users alike is the sharing of random thoughts. This is both a pro and con to Twitter as a platform. Users comment on everything from the traffic and weather to their personal daily thoughts and inspirations. These random posts can help users get a good feel for what is going on with the people in their network. Depending on who users choose to follow they will get a vastly different experience. Those who choose to follow only official news sources and some of their professional colleagues will likely get a more professional-feeling experience when they look at their personal feed. Following famous people and friends will be completely different. Users can stop following other accounts at any time, so they can adjust the type of posts they see if they are not enjoying them.

Accessing and tracking news from multiple sources appeals to many Twitter users. For example, someone who is interested in both politics and astronomy can choose to follow prominent astronomers like Neil deGrasse Tyson, as well as their local mayor, state senator, and even the president of the United States. Tweets from prominent people are often featured on television news and other media; even news agencies now follow public and political figures on Twitter to keep up on the very latest information.

TWITTER TERMINOLOGY

Blocking—Blocking another account blocks that user from following an account or viewing that account's tweets. Blocking that account will not notify that user, but they may notice that they can no longer access the account.

Bots—Twitter Bots are "robot" programs that control Twitter accounts through the Twitter application programming interface (API), a set of functions that allows special access to Twitter functionality. There are always bots on Twitter, which can be confusing to some users who may think that their posts are from real people. Instead, they are posts automated by the bot software in response to keywords or other settings. Twitter bots can be fun, informational, or problematic. For example, anyone who tweets posts using the words *socialist* or *communist* may get a response from @RedScareBot, a bot using the persona of former U.S. senator Joseph McCarthy. The Twitter bot @MikeMovies exists only to tweet at actor Val Kilmer, encouraging him to make more movies. These are relatively benign and funny. More problematic bots instigate arguments or respond to political or social issues. Twitter removes bots that harass users or cause problems.

Direct Message (DM)—If a Twitter user wants to send a message to another Twitter user privately, they send a direct message or "DM" to that user. To send a direct message, click on the linked username for the person to go to their profile page. Click on the Message button in the left column. If a user has turned off the ability to receive direct messages, then the button will not appear.

Feed/Timeline—Each Twitter user has their own feed or timeline, which shows them the personalized list of tweets from followers they have chosen. This includes things that their followers retweet. The feed will also occasionally show "promoted" tweets, which are paid advertisements.

Follow/Follower—Twitter users can follow other accounts so that their posts appear in their personalized feed. Users do not need to follow everyone who follows them. Anyone can follow a public account, whether or not they know that person. Users who want to limit who can follow their posts should create a private account.

Handle or Username—A Twitter username or handle is the unique name you have chosen on the platform. It will always start with an @ symbol, and no two users can have the same name. Users can also put in an expanded name in their profile, which can be changed at any time, but once you have chosen a handle, it usually stays the same. Many people choose their real name if it is not already taken. For example, the actor Patton Oswalt uses the handle @pattonoswalt so that he is easily recognizable. If you choose to use your real name and are posting publicly, be aware that it may be easier for strangers to identify you from your account and posts. Twitter users who want to remain anonymous should choose a username appropriately. If you do want to change your username, you can, but that can be confusing to people who follow you. In addition, anywhere you put your handle (such as on a business card or in an e-mail) will no longer be correct.

Hashtag—A hashtag refers to a keyword or phrase without spaces that starts with a hash/number [#] symbol in front of it. Hashtags help people find tweets on the same topic or from the same event. Events and conferences usually have a designated hashtag that is recommended for attendees. Searching for that unique hashtag allows people to follow along with the happenings at the event, from the participants' point of view. Hashtags can also help people identify important topics or trends. Hashtags automatically get linked on Twitter. Clicking on a linked hashtag in a tweet or searching for it in the search box will show all tweets that use the same hashtag.

Mute—Muting an account stops tweets from that account from showing up in your feed. Users can mute an account that they follow if they want to stay connected to that person but don't want to see their tweets. They can also mute an account they don't follow if they don't want to see anything that their friends may retweet from that account. Some people mute accounts temporarily if a user is tweeting a lot about a certain event or issue. Muting an account will not notify that user.

Reply—Users can post a reply to any tweet by using the small reply icon under that tweet. The icon looks like a conversation bubble. The reply will appear under the original tweet and will also show up to the replier's followers.

Retweet—Twitter users can retweet other users' tweets, which means reposting another's post to that users' followers. The retweet icon, which looks like two arrows in a circle, appears below every tweet. A number beside the retweet icon shows how many times the post has been retweeted. The person retweeting can choose to add their own comments, or not.

Tag or Mention—Twitter users can mention or tag another Twitter user by using their handle (for example @scalzi) in a tweet. The person using that handle will receive a notice that they were tagged. Separating the @ symbol from the rest of the handle with a space is a way to mention someone without sending them a tag notice.

Thread—Tweets that have multiple replies, responses, and comments, or tweets that have multiple follow-up tweets, are called a thread. You can follow the thread to see the full conversation. A link for "Show this thread" will appear below a tweet if a thread conversation is available. Thread may also be used to describe when people post a series of tweets that are intended to be read in series, usually because they cannot fit their full message in the 280-character limit. They may use numbers to indicate that the tweet is one of two tweets in a series (1/2), second of three (2/3), and so on.

Tweet—A tweet is a message or post that you create and share on Twitter. Tweets are limited to 280 characters and can contain photos, links, and other media.

Verified—Twitter accounts with a blue check mark icon next to their screen name and handle have been *verified* as being who they claim to be. Businesses, public officials, and others who may be copied online get verified so that people know which account is real. Twitter only verifies accounts that are identified as "public interest."[2]

THE BASICS OF USING TWITTER

Setting up a new Twitter account is straightforward and similar to setting up an account on many other platforms. The most difficult part is likely to be choosing a Twitter username, or *handle*. A Twitter handle usually stays the same even if other things in a user profile change: it is like a unique address that leads to that account only. Because it is short (limited to 15 characters) and unique, it can be challenging for new users to think of something that no one else in the world has chosen. Give a little bit of thought to what you want to use and be ready to add numbers or change the spelling if needed. You can technically change your username after creating your account, but that can cause some confusion if you have connected with a lot of people who are used to your other name. It is much easier and less confusing to change the account display name: the 50-character name that displays in your account, above or next to your handle. The display name can be your full name, if your name was not available as a handle. It can also be anything else that you want: a Halloween-themed name in October, or a funny moniker like Becky "Gets Stuff Done" Martinez.

To set up a new account, go to http://twitter.com and click on the Sign Up menu option. Users are required to have either a phone number or an e-mail address linked to their account. An e-mail address can only be linked to one Twitter account at any time, so if you have a previous Twitter account or a work account that you manage, it will need to be disabled or changed to a new address. Twitter will text or e-mail a numeric code to the provided contact address in order to confirm that it is correct and real. After confirming the code, new users create a password and start creating their account. Twitter will suggest topics of interest (see figure 3.2), and specific people to follow, but you can click Skip for Now and Next if you want to get to the main Account screen.

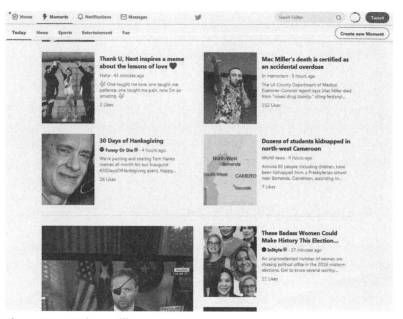

Figure 3.2.   Twitter will suggest topics to new users.

The main account screen that Twitter users will see when they log in, whether on mobile or desktop, is their personalized *feed* or *timeline*. Figure 3.3 shows the mobile view of the feed, while figure 3.4 shows the desktop view of the home timeline with all the main features identified. This personalized feed will show tweets, likes, and retweets from the people that the Twitter account holder has chosen to follow. In addition, it will show some promoted tweets: these are paid advertisements promoted by Twitter. Promoted advertisements will be targeted to the account holder in some way, sometimes based on the hashtags used or keywords in the account profile.[3] That means that some promoted materials may look an awful lot like tweets from followers. Twitter users can keep an eye out for the word *Promoted* next to an arrow icon at the bottom of a tweet to know for sure whether a tweet was from a follower or advertiser. Tweets that are retweeted or liked by followers will say so at the top of the tweet.

Figure 3.3. View of a Twitter account feed using the Twitter application on a mobile device.

Figure 3.4. View of a Twitter account feed on a computer.

Due to the constantly changing nature of Twitter, the timeline isn't really meant to be read in its entirety. In fact, it is usually impossible to reach the end of the feed unless you follow a small amount of people who do not tweet much. The feed will continue to scroll down without ever reaching a bottom, with new tweets constantly added to the top. This large influx of information is difficult for some new Twitter users who may be accustomed to reading all the things posted in a social media account. It is one of the key ways that Twitter is different, and it is one of the benefits. It does require users to wrap their minds around the fact that they can only ever get a point-in-time of what is going on. Still, users who are overwhelmed by the amount of posts on their feed can control their timeline in several ways that may help make it more manageable.

Posts on the timeline can either be set in reverse chronological order (newest first) or ordered by the setting "Show the Best Tweets First," which can be turned on and off. The nonchronological option is on by default. It is available in the account settings and can be reached by clicking on the tiny profile photo in the upper right (desktop) or right (mobile) and choosing Settings and Privacy. Keeping the box checked for Timeline: Show the Best Tweets First option will mean that Twitter chooses what goes at the top of the feed based on what the user is most likely to care about. That includes tweets from accounts that the user interacts with the most and tweets that are popular with followers and other connections.[4]

Another way to control what does and does not show up in a home Twitter feed is the use of *muting*. Accounts or specific words can be muted in the Settings and Privacy menu. This means that those accounts, words, phrases, or hashtags will not appear in the timeline once they are chosen by the account holder, even if they are tweeted by someone they follow. Muting an account will mean that nothing that person tweets or retweets will appear. Muting specific words, phrases, hashtags, or even usernames will prevent any tweet or retweet from showing up. This can be used strategically to turn off notifications for a short time when a news event is going on, or it can be used to more permanently remove certain things from view if the account holder just does not want to see that sort of tweet. Be aware: muting common words will sometimes unintentionally block tweets that aren't really about the intended targets so choose muted words carefully. It is also easy to forget that words have been muted, so checking on your muted settings periodically is recommended. If you want to avoid seeing nudity, violence, and other potentially offensive content from all sources, Twitter has an option in the Settings and Privacy > Privacy and Safety menu that allows users to hide sensitive content.

It is worthwhile to look through all the available Twitter settings when you open a new account in order to adjust things like notifications, security options, and preferences. By clicking on the tiny profile photo in the upper right (desktop) or left (mobile) and choosing Settings and Privacy, you will see a list of options in the left sidebar, shown in figure 3.5. Each of the options opens a new menu of individual controls and settings to choose from.

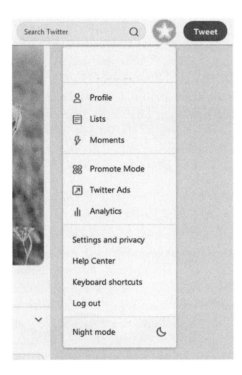

Figure 3.5. Twitter Settings and Privacy options.

Some Available Settings Options

- Request a downloadable file of your entire Twitter archive including all of your tweets (available in Settings and Privacy > Account)
- Turning video autoplay on and off (available in Settings and Privacy > Account)
- Adjust e-mail notifications so that you do or do not get e-mail when certain Twitter activities occur (available in Settings and Privacy > Email Notifications)
- Search for existing contacts who have Twitter accounts by uploading contacts from Google or Outlook (available in Settings and Privacy > Find Friends)

- Add the ability to add image descriptions when posting images (available in Settings and Privacy > Accessibility)
- Turn on night mode to reduce eye strain (available by clicking on your profile image > Night Mode)

Managing Your Profile

Clicking on the small profile photo in the upper right (desktop) or left (mobile) and choosing Profile will take users to their profile view. This view shows the account holder's profile description and photo, header, tweet activity, and tweets. Click on Edit Profile to allow editing the header and profile photo, profile name, profile bio, location, linked website, birthday, and theme color. Profile bios are limited to just 160 characters, so be brief in describing yourself and your interests. Remember, though, that anything you list may be used for promoted advertising. Also, if your account is public, remember that your co-workers and family may stumble across your account whether or not you invite them to look.

How to Tweet

Tweeting is easy. Whether you are using the desktop version shown in figure 3.6, or the mobile version shown in figure 3.7, you can click the tweet button and a text box will appear. On the desktop version, you can also click into the box at the top of the feed where it asks, "What's happening?" The icons at the bottom of the tweet box allow you to add a photo, GIF, survey/poll, or your location (unless you have turned that option off). You can also add an emoji by using your mobile emoji keyboard or the smiley face icon in the text box if you are on a computer. If you go over the 280-character limit, the text will be colored red, and a number will appear to let you know how far over you have gone. You can sometimes reduce the character count by using abbreviations,

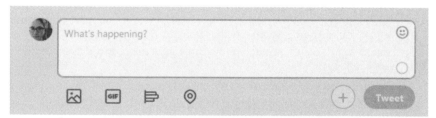

Figure 3.6.   Tweeting from the Twitter website on a computer.

Figure 3.7. Tweeting from the Twitter application on a mobile device.

symbols, and numbers instead of spelling everything out. There are also many articles online that give tips and tricks for how to craft great tweets.

But I Don't Want to Tweet

Some people choose to browse or "lurk" on Twitter and don't want to post or retweet anything. Unfortunately, Twitter designates accounts that have not tweeted in six months as inactive.[5] If you are primarily using Twitter to browse, you may want to consider tweeting sporadically to avoid being inactive. There is some risk that inactive accounts may be locked by Twitter during purges intended to remove bots or other accounts that are not real people. Usually users can turn the account back on quickly by following a link, but it can be disruptive and annoying to have to do this.

Notifications

The notifications screen shows you the interaction that your tweets have on the platform, for example, when others like, retweet, or comment on your posts. Direct messages will trigger a notification. You can also see when other users mention you by including your username/handle in a tweet. On mobile, you can reach the notification screen by clicking on the bell icon at the bottom of the screen. On desktop, you can click Notifications at the top of the screen. When you have notifications that you have not viewed yet, number icons will appear to let you know how many you have.

Searching and Browsing

Once someone has mastered their own timeline feed, they may want to explore what else is available on Twitter. You can always search for hashtags, keywords, locations, or news events in the search box. Results will default to the "Top" options, which usually means the most popular or most viewed results. The items that appear are not always the most current information on a topic, just the most popular. You can change the option to "Latest" to see up-to-the-minute information about your search topic. If you are looking for an active news event, this is usually the option you want. You can also choose to specifically search for people, photos, videos, news, and live broadcasts. Once you have chosen one of those options, you can limit even further by using search filters. Search filter options are available in the upper left on a computer view or can be accessed on mobile by choosing the sliding bar icon next to the search field. These filters can help you limit mentions on this topic to people you follow, or from people tweeting near to you.

You can also browse Twitter by viewing and following trends. Trends are popular topics that people in a certain region are talking about. They can be hashtags or just words and phrases that are being used a lot at that point in time. Because trends are created automatically based on use, they don't always make sense and sometimes duplicate one another by being slightly different takes on the same topic. On mobile, you can see current trends by clicking on the search icon. You do not need to choose anything to search to see the trends: they appear as news "For You." You can scroll down to see more trends. On a computer view, trends will appear in the left sidebar below the profile box and follow suggestions. If a trend has been identified by Twitter, there may be a short description underneath it to explain its appearance (see figure 3.8). Other trends are not explained and may list the number of recent tweets about the topic underneath. Trends are clickable, so you can easily click through if you would like to know why the term is trending.

You can create tailored trends to your location if you would like to see more specific (or more broad) results. For example, you can choose United States or worldwide to see those trends, or most larger cities. Smaller cities often don't have enough use to show trends. Be aware, if you set the trends to worldwide you are likely to see many trends that are not in the English language.

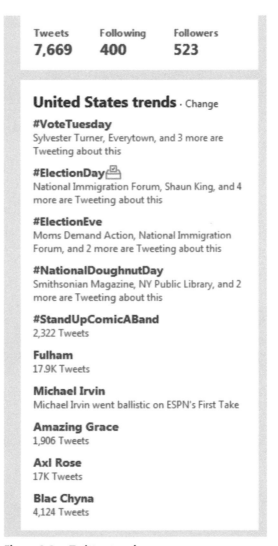

Figure 3.8. Twitter trends.

PRIVACY AND SAFETY

Twitter offers a lot of information about privacy and many options for users who want to manage their privacy and safety while using the platform. Twitter has a privacy policy that is available to read online or download as a PDF. It is linked in the menu below Trends on the desktop view or from Settings and Privacy > About Twitter in the mobile app. Many safety and security settings are available and adjustable in a Twitter account. It is worth reviewing them whether you have a new account or have had an account for years, since they do change.

Twitter has many privacy and security concerns. Twitter regularly receives criticism that it does not do enough to curb the frequent online harassment that takes place on the platform.[6] While users agree to not participate in abusive behavior, Twitter is a large public platform, which makes it hard to police. Inappropriate or harassing tweets or comments can be sent to Twitter by clicking on the down arrow in any tweet and selecting the Report Tweet menu option. Any online networking site is likely to have some issues with harassment, trolling, or abuse, but it should not prevent people from using the sites. The down-arrow menu in each tweet also offers options to block or mute the user, which happens immediately and does not depend on Twitter acting. On the positive side, photos posted to the site may suggest a location to tag but will not retain any specific location data when the photo is posted. This can prevent strangers from tracking your location, including your home.

Some of Twitter's Safety and Security Options

- Use the option in Settings and Privacy > Account to require personal information in order to reset your password.
- Use the option in Settings and Privacy > Account to require additional verification at login.
- Settings and Privacy > Privacy and Safety offers options to create a private Twitter account. By turning on the "Tweet privacy," setting only approved followers can see tweets.
- Turn off an account's ability to receive direct messages from anyone in the Settings and Privacy > Privacy and Safety menu.

Twitter Safety Tips

- If you have the Tweet with a Location menu option turned on in Settings and Privacy > Privacy and Safety, only use it in public places.

- Delete location data from previous posts by going to Privacy and Safety > Tweet Location > Delete Location Information and save.
- Regularly review account settings, especially the Privacy and Safety menu.
- If you have an anonymized username and profile and do not want to be easily identified by those who know you in person, you may want to make it impossible for people to search for you using a phone number or e-mail address in the Settings and Privacy > Privacy and Safety menu.
- Over time, many users allow other applications or accounts to access their Twitter account. For example, bloggers or Instagram users may link their accounts to make tweeting easier. Review the accounts that have access to your Twitter account in the Settings and Privacy > Apps and Devices menu.
- Do not add birthday or location to profile information.
- Do not use the Show When I'm LIVE menu option in your profile settings.

SPECIAL FEATURES

Twitter Analytics is a tracking and statistics dashboard that is built into the platform. It is free and automatically available to all Twitter users. Analytics can be reached by clicking on the profile image and then Analytics. You can also get there by clicking on the graph available when viewing your profile page. Analytics provides more information than most basic users want to know, but it can be interesting to look at statistics such as average number of retweets over the past 28 days, number of impressions (the number of times your tweet appears on other people's timelines), and most popular tweets. Twitter analytics is also very visually stimulating, with many graphs and images, as is shown in figure 3.9.

Third-Party Apps and interaction are common on Twitter. Because it is so widely used, Twitter is well integrated with websites and other social media across the internet. Users with blogs or their own websites will usually have a plugin available that allows them to link their posts to Twitter, so that other people can share from their site. Instagram users have the option to post any photo to Twitter at the same time it is posted on Instagram. Most news websites have an option to tweet out individual articles as well: just look for the tiny blue bird icon on the article page.

Help Center is linked from the menu below Trends or from the Settings menu in the mobile app. The Twitter Help Center is a very robust website devoted to helping Twitter users understand the platform and manage their

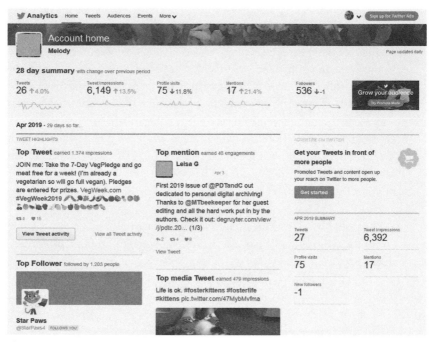

Figure 3.9. Twitter analytics shows account statistics.

profiles. It has the most current news and help on the platform's features and offers a search bar to search the whole help center easily. It also has contact options, including messaging and filing a problem report. It is the best place to start for everything from tips on feed management to information on current research Twitter is conducting.

YOUTUBE

YouTube is a video-sharing platform where users can share and watch videos on almost any topic. Anyone can watch publicly posted videos without having an account, but account holders can additionally post videos, add comments, rate videos, save favorites, and create private videos to share. Creating an account and logging in will also allow YouTube to suggest videos that viewers may enjoy, based on their previous search and viewing history. Users who create an account can also create a video channel, where others can follow their posts and activity. If a video channel reaches a high level of popularity, it can be monetized: that means that it can start receiving advertising revenue from ads attached to the channel and videos. The most popularly viewed videos on YouTube (most are music videos) have been watched billions of times by audiences across the world.[1]

WHY DO PEOPLE USE YOUTUBE?

YouTube is the largest video-sharing platform on the planet and one of the most popular social media platforms available.[2] Whether you are looking for a notable clip from a movie or television show, want a tutorial for a new video game, or are looking for videos of kittens meowing loudly, YouTube is a good place to start. Because of integration with Google and other search options, searching the internet for any term and then choosing to view videos will almost always include videos from YouTube. You do not even need to navigate to the YouTube website to view the video since most play directly in the search results. YouTube videos can be easily shared and embedded on other websites, so chances are that most internet users have viewed videos from YouTube at some point.

The most common way that people use YouTube is simply watching videos. Many users never create or post a video. Instead, they browse or search for videos to watch and interact by commenting and sharing. Whether for entertainment or education, it is easy to search for videos on the platform, with or without an account. Those who use YouTube a lot or want to interact on the platform will want an account so that they can use the extra features. The most basic account features include liking/disliking a video, commenting on a video, saving it to watch later, or saving it as a favorite. Video watchers can also subscribe to a channel, so they can be notified later when a new video is added by the same creator.

With more than one billion videos on YouTube, posting videos is obviously a big part of the platform, too. Anyone can upload videos to YouTube and gain a following. Video creators range from professional or famous, to college students with a recurring vlog (video blog), and to people who only ever post one random funny video they took with their phone. Videos can be uploaded directly from a phone or can be created and enhanced using video software before posting. YouTube Studio has a free video editor available, and it even offers free music and sound clips that can be added to video creations. Video creators can add keywords, descriptions, and titles to increase attention to their videos. Those who post multiple videos can see their uploads and track use, likes, and other statistics through their channel's dashboard and analytics.

YouTube users can also create private or unlisted videos where they share personal creations with family, friends, or other limited audiences. Videos posted privately cannot be viewed by just anyone: viewers must have a Google account and be invited to view the videos. Private videos will not appear in search results or video recommendations. Unlisted videos also do not appear in search results but can be viewed by anyone with a link to the video. Private options make it safer for people to post family or personal videos without fear that unknown people will be able to see things like their Christmas morning or child's birthday.

YouTube can also be a professional tool. There are a lot of professional and famous people sharing content on YouTube. Companies also share content, including music videos, advertisements, and promotional skits. Organizations like universities and nonprofits may share news or projects with video posts on YouTube. Companies may also create learning content, such as tutorials for how to use their products or videos from conferences they hosted. Individuals who want to use YouTube as a professional tool might create an online professional introduction or portfolio that introduces them to potential employers. Sharing links and videos for professional uses can be done privately, such as with class participants, or publicly to anyone who wants to watch. Watchers/ viewers do not need to have a Google or YouTube account to watch private videos that you create.

Many YouTube creators hope to eventually monetize their account. Monetization means that they will gain enough followers and views so that they can add advertising to their videos and make money. To be eligible to apply to the YouTube Partner Program for monetization, creators must have more than 1,000 subscribers and more than 4,000 hours of viewing in the previous 12 months. Once they become partners, users can make money when people view their videos with advertising attached.[3]

There are videos about a lot of things on YouTube, but some categories have become especially popular on the platform. Here are some common YouTube video types:

- Challenges—Challenge videos record a person accepting something as a challenge to perform some task, such as eating a spoon full of cinnamon or a hot pepper. Some challenges are inspirational. For example, many people dumped ice water over their heads to raise money for amyotrophic lateral sclerosis during the ice bucket challenge. However, YouTube has also been home to challenge videos that are bizarre and potentially harmful. In early 2019, YouTube banned videos of challenges it deems dangerous.[4] Watchers should keep in mind that any challenge video posted on YouTube may be staged/fake.
- Fails—These are videos of people falling, hurting themselves, or otherwise attempting things that do not work out. Clips of people missing easy game show answers and dogs walking into glass doors are among the many available fail videos on YouTube.
- Fashion and Style—Many videos brand themselves as OOTD (outfit of the day) or GRWM (Get Ready with Me). Viewers can follow along with fashionable video creators as they do their hair and makeup, decide on outfits, and share their style. Fashion and style is a huge part of YouTube, and searching for style topics will yield many search results (see figure 4.1).
- Reactions—In reaction videos, users film people's reactions to emotional or unexpected events, for example, recording someone watching a suspenseful television show or reacting to a family member visiting unexpectedly. The person reacting may or may not know that they are being

☰ ▶ YouTube   🔍 ⬆ ⊞ 🧭 🔔 ◯

≡ FILTER

How to Create a Glowing Makeup Look with a ⋮

Create A Glowing Makeup Look with A Bold Red Pout for Spring!

3:53

MY MAKEUP COLLECTION &
PatrickStarrr ✔ 284K views • 1 day ago

YES YES YES! I love watching organizing videos and being nosy in DRAWERS and I

New

26:07

Best Makeup Transformations 2019
PASSION MAKEUP •
762K views • 3 weeks ago

Best Makeup Transformations 2019 New Makeup Tutorials Compilation Instagram

10:46

The Top Viral Makeup Videos On Instagram 😎
Beauty Club • 5.9M views • 1 year ago

Perfect Makeup: Best Makeup App for Looking Flawless: http://bit.ly

12:41

I SPENT $500 ON A FULL FACE OF TJMAXX
Manny Mua ✔ 323K views • 1 day ago

Figure 4.1. Style topics make up a large part of YouTube.

recorded, and what they are watching may be included in a smaller screen in the video.

- Reviews—Whether it's a teenage girl reviewing a new movie, a young man reviewing a vacuum, or Hugh Grant reviewing his own film appearances, reviews of things new and old are popular on YouTube.
- Tutorials—Tutorials for video games and software are popular, but YouTube has tutorials on many topics. For example, you can learn how to apply makeup, how to medicate a kitten, how to fly-fish, or how to snake a drain.
- Unboxing / Unpacking / Assembly—These videos follow users as they unpack and put together (or otherwise figure out) new things they have acquired. Video creators can share their frustration and first thoughts as they assemble a new printer or a children's doll house.

YOUTUBE TERMINOLOGY

AMA—AMA or "ask me anything" videos are interviews where famous or interesting people answer questions about their lives and experiences. These are often cross-marketed on Reddit, where AMA is very popular.

Cards—Cards are a way to add interactive features to a video after it is uploaded to your channel. Creators can add cards by going to the video manager and choosing Add Card next to the video to be annotated (see figure 4.2). Cards replaced video annotations, which used to be viewable on computers but not mobile devices. Cards are available on both.

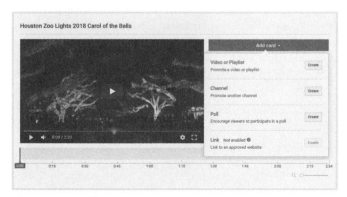

Figure 4.2. Adding a card.

Channel—This is the term used to describe the main page where a creator's videos will appear on YouTube. A channel can be customized with different backgrounds. Users can have multiple accounts that have their own video channel and can switch between them by clicking on their profile image and selecting Switch Account. Businesses can also have channels.

Collab—This term is short for *collaboration* and is used when one YouTube user creates a video featuring another YouTube user. It is a way for two YouTube video creators to help one another gain popularity and a cross-following. It could also be called cross-promotion.

Community—This is the common term used to describe everyone on YouTube.

DITL—An acronym for Day in the Life, this term is often used to describe a video where someone is talking about their daily routine.

Endslate / Endscreen—This is the screen at the end of a video that recommends additional videos that the watcher may want to see. Often they are videos on the same channel or those with similar topics or keywords.

Influencer—A YouTube influencer is someone who has built a significant following on the platform. Influencers have thousands of subscribers, and their videos have high numbers of views and comments. Influencers often monetize their channels to make money and may participate in additional tie-ins with advertisers or promoters.

GRWM—An acronym short for Get Ready with Me, GRWM is used for videos of people getting ready for their day, usually doing their hair and makeup and making fashion and style choices.

Like / Dislike—Thumbs up (like) and thumbs down (dislike) options appear below every video on YouTube. Users who are logged in can share their opinion about a video by clicking on one of the icons. Whether you like or dislike a video may impact how often you see content from the same channel in the future. Users can also like or dislike comments by other users.

Miniplayer—This is a video play option that you can select when watching a video. It will reduce the viewing size of the video so that it plays only on a small part of the screen.

Monetize / Monetization—Users whose channels have more than 1,000 subscribers and more than 4,000 hours of viewing time in the previous 12 months can monetize, meaning they can make money from advertising on their videos.

Prank—Similar to a social experiment, a prank is when a video creator tests people in some way and catches it all on camera. Pranks tend to be more lighthearted or pointless than social experiments. For example, a prank may show people's reactions to eating a cake that looks like a regular cake but turns out to be filled with pickles. They are similar to many April Fool's Day jokes.

OOTD—Short for Outfit of the Day, OOTD videos show someone's fashion choices for that day. Usually these videos are in series, with someone showing off multiple outfits on their channel.

Save—This is an option that appears below YouTube videos. It allows users who are logged in to save the video to a "watch later" list, favorites, or to a new playlist.

Share—This is an option that appears below YouTube videos.

Social Experiment—Similar to a prank, a social experiment video shows how people (often strangers or people on the street) react to something. For example, a person could walk by a crowd and drop their wallet to see whether people pick it up or return it as a test of their honesty. YouTube social experiments have received a lot of criticism for being staged/not real.

Studio / Creator Studio—YouTube's Creator Studio is where users manage their channel and videos. To get to the studio, go to https://studio.youtube.com/.

Thumbnail / Custom Thumbnail—A thumbnail is the tiny view of a video that users see before they click on the video to watch. Often it is the first frame of the video, but it can also be a custom thumbnail, which the creator chose to highlight.

Unboxing—Unboxing is the act of unpacking a newly acquired item on film and sharing early reactions with a YouTube audience.

Verified—YouTube users and channels can be verified by providing a phone number that links to their account. A text or call to that number will provide verification. Verified accounts have more options, including the ability to post videos longer than 15 minutes, choose custom thumbnails, and get a Verified badge on their account page.

Vlogs / Vlogging—Vlogging (video blogging) is the act of sharing thoughts or feelings or details about daily activities in video form. Vloggers who post often may gain a following as people get to know them and feel invested in their lives and experiences.

THE BASICS OF USING YOUTUBE

YouTube was purchased by Google in 2006 and requires a Google ID in order to create an account (again, viewing public videos does not require an account or Google ID).[5] If you already have a Google account, you can just log in to any

Google feature (Gmail, Google Docs, etc.), or you can navigate to YouTube .com and log in using the same account information. If you do not already have a Google account, you can create one easily. Using Google tools and creating a Google account does not mean that you have to use Gmail—this is a common misconception. You can log in to Google using any e-mail address and can access Google tools, including YouTube, with that login.

Searching or browsing videos is easy, and more features are available when a user is logged in. The search bar can be used to search for video names or keywords. YouTube will suggest words as they are typed into the search bar to help users find videos they want. Once search results appear, video watchers can select Filter to see options for limiting search results (see figure 4.3). Some of the filters include video duration, date uploaded, features, and rating. Users can also browse videos by going to YouTube and seeing what is trending (popular at the moment). Logged-in watchers can also see customized content on their home screen without searching, including videos recommended to them based on their previous viewing history.

Video watchers have several options when viewing a video. The viewing options are similar on a browser or mobile device. However, on a mobile device some viewing options may be hidden unless you click on the video screen or a

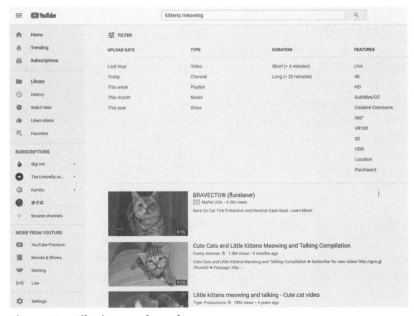

Figure 4.3. Filtering search results.

down arrow that shows additional choices (see figure 4.4). Logged-in users can indicate that they like or dislike a video by clicking on the thumbs up or thumbs down icons. They can see the total likes and dislikes from other users next to each icon. Users can also share the video via other social media platforms or by copying a link for the video, which they can then e-mail or text. Videos can also be saved to a favorites or watch list by clicking on the +Save option. On a mobile device, users can click on the video as it plays to see options for volume control or for expanding the video to full screen. Those using a browser window on a computer can choose full screen, theater mode (which fills the screen within the browser window), or miniplayer (which shows the video in the lower right-hand corner of the screen). Miniplayer can be used to watch a video on the side while you browse or work on something else.

My Channel and YouTube Studio offer information and access for video creators. Clicking on your profile image and choosing My Channel will show YouTube creators their own videos, channels, and playlists but with limited options. To create and manage videos users can choose YouTube Studio instead.

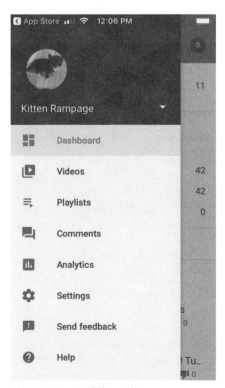

Figure 4.4.   Mobile options.

YouTube Studio is where content creators on YouTube go to create, upload, and manage their videos. Users who do not have many videos uploaded will usually see ideas and suggestions from YouTube, including tips and tutorials for managing a YouTube channel. You can also get to YouTube Studio at any time by navigating directly to studio.youtube.com.

YouTube Studio has multiple sections and, although it is still part of YouTube, feels more like a toolkit than a social media site. While in the studio, YouTube users don't usually see other people's videos or advertisements. Instead, it is a place for users to see and work on their own videos. When first navigating to YouTube Studio, it will open to the dashboard. This is where recent videos, news, and recent analytics (usage statistics) will appear. Clicking the Videos menu option in the sidebar will show all of a user's videos in a list view, with details including privacy setting, date posted, views, comments, and likes (see figure 4.5). Clicking Analytics will show details of how many times videos are watched, top videos, latest activity, and other custom reports. Other features available in the studio include channel customization options and an audio library of free sounds to use in videos (see figure 4.6). The mobile app version of YouTube Studio is called YT Studio and offers many of the same features from a mobile phone.

To upload a video to YouTube from the browser version of YouTube Studio, click the video camera icon with a + sign inside of it. You can choose to live stream or upload a video. The choice to make a video public, unlisted, private,

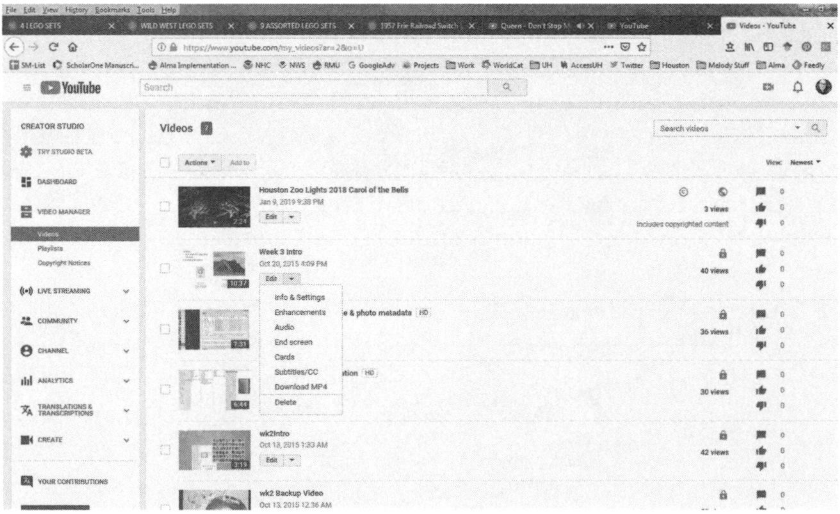

Figure 4.5.   YouTube Videos menu.

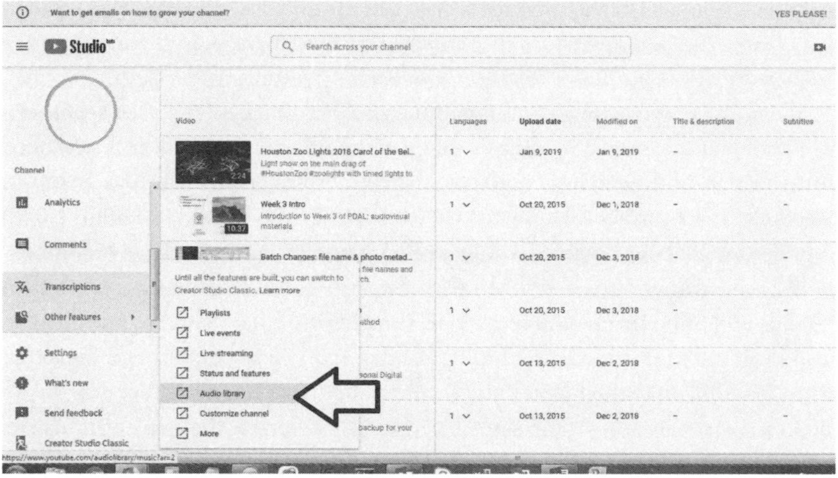

Figure 4.6. YouTube studio audio library.

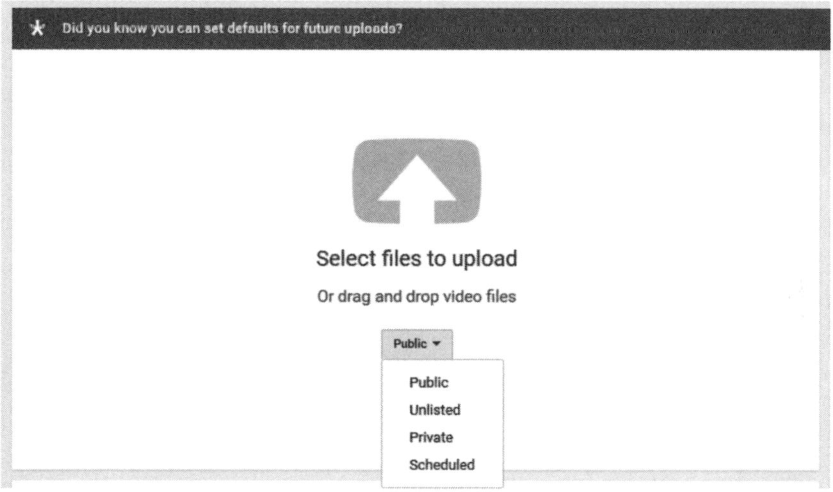

Figure 4.7. Drag and drop video files for upload.

or scheduled happens right at upload, so users can make that choice right up front. Once they select the privacy setting, users can drag the video right onto the screen where it says to drag and drop files (see figure 4.7). Users will have the chance to add a description, keywords, and other details about their video. When uploading a new video, consider what keywords users will use that might lead to that video. Having good keywords and a good video title are important to building a YouTube audience, and there are many tutorials online that can help. If a channel is being used to always post the same sorts of videos, the channel creator can add keywords that will appear by default in each video to save time later. That option is available in the account settings.

To find account settings on a computer browser, click on the user profile image and then the gear icon. The Settings menu offers many easy and advanced features that both watchers and content creators might use. In the Settings: Account screen, users can create a new channel, sign up for premium (paid) services, or change account settings like contact details. In Settings > Notifications, users can choose how often they hear from YouTube and what sorts of e-mails and announcements they want to receive. Other Settings options can also be found in this menu, including history and privacy details and apps that users have linked to their YouTube account. Terms of Use and Help can always be found at the bottom of the screen. On a mobile device, the same options can be found in the three-dot menu in the upper right of the screen > Settings.

PRIVACY AND SAFETY

Safety is a concern for YouTube since it is easy to share a lot of personal information with a video. While many of the same safety rules for all social media apply to YouTube (don't show expensive belongings, don't show your address, etc.), YouTube users may not realize how much detail about their lives can easily be shared in the background of videos they post. Before posting a video, creators should review it and consider whether anything in the background could make them a target for theft or make it easy for others to locate their home. Since videos sometimes go viral and get heavily shared, it is not impossible that a funny video could be the focus of discussion by thousands of people. So, video creators should be cautious, especially when vlogging or posting personal experiences.

Anyone viewing YouTube videos should also consider the source and reputability of a video creator. YouTube does not check the validity or truthfulness of the videos' claims, so the platform has a lot of misinformation. Even videos that seem reputable may not be. Make sure to double-check any concerning or sensational claims with a trusted source rather than assuming a video is telling the truth. Similarly, many videos (including challenges, pranks, and social experiments) may be completely false. These videos may show something happening that looks like a random event caught on film, when in fact it was staged. In some cases, fake challenges may encourage people to try something risky that isn't a good idea. YouTube recently changed its community guidelines on challenge videos that present physical harm and banned them from the site in early 2019.[6]

YouTube does not allow pornography, harassment, hate speech, and "incitement to violence" in either the videos and comments on the platform. However, those rules are hard to police due to the size of the site and the large volume of videos that are constantly added. YouTube depends on users and technology to find content that violates their rules. Parents and others who worry about this sort of content should be cautious when they use the site, and report abuses if they encounter them. The Report option is in the three-dot menu that appears under each video so it is easy to report content violations as soon as you see them.

Some Safety Tips for YouTube

- For your own legal protection and to maintain your good standing on the site, do not post copyrighted materials on the site unless you know the video you are posting meets fair use standards. For more information on fair use, visit YouTube's Fair Use information page at www.youtube.com/yt/about/copyright/fair-use/.
- Users can click on their profile image > Settings (gear icon) > History and Privacy to choose whether their likes and subscriptions are private.
- Remember, the term *unlisted* does not mean private. An unlisted video cannot be found in YouTube search results, but anyone who has the link can see an unlisted video. Users who create unlisted videos and share the link should assume that others may share the link as well. Avoid posting sensitive or personal videos as unlisted. Use private instead.
- Be conscious of your video's background. Always be aware of what and who is behind you on camera. Home videos, including videos where you can clearly see an address number of homes where people currently live, are best kept private. Creators can change privacy levels of any video by going to their YouTube Studio Dashboard, clicking Videos and changing the visibility next to a video from Public to Private (see figure 4.8).

SPECIAL FEATURES AND HELP

Live streaming is available on YouTube as well. That means that users who want to release a video to YouTube live, as it is happening, can do so. To use live streaming, YouTube creators should go to YouTube Studio and click Enable in the Live Streaming option box. Enabling for the first time may take 24 hours before the feature is available. For live streaming to be an option, a chan-

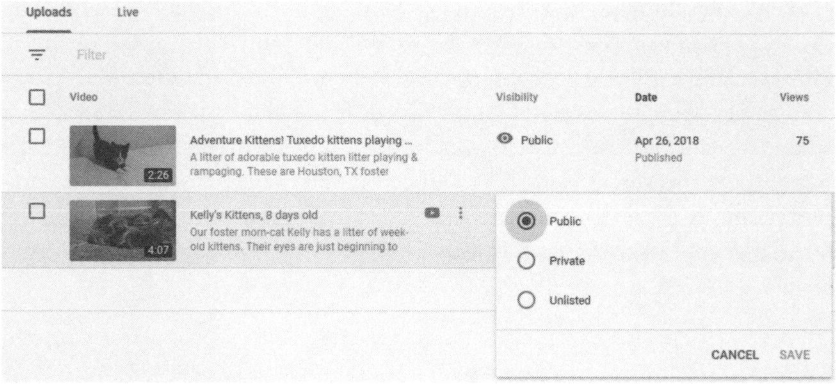

Figure 4.8.   Change privacy of a video.

nel must be verified and have no live stream restrictions from the previous 90 days. Users can live stream from a computer web camera or from their mobile app. Tutorials and directions are available through YouTube Help.

Dark Theme is a browser viewing option on YouTube that may help to reduce eye strain when viewing videos at night. By turning on Dark Theme, the white areas of the YouTube page turn dark. This function can be toggled on and off easily by clicking on the user's profile icon and choosing Dark Theme, then toggling to On or Off.

SNAPCHAT

Snapchat is a mobile messaging platform that has become popular with teens and young adults because of its built-in photo editing and privacy defaults. Snapchat is only for mobile devices. It is also a relatively private social media platform compared to the other popular sites and apps: Snapchat posts, including chat and images, generally disappear on both the sender and receiver end after they have been viewed. This means that there is not a "feed" to view on someone's Snapchat account, which is a major difference from most social media. For users who like to save things, this platform may be frustrating, although there are a few options for saving things if you do it up front. However, many people appear to enjoy the lack of accounts and saved posts since it does not feel overwhelming. Because it has marketed itself as a more private platform, Snapchat additionally informs you if someone uses a screen capture to save something that you have sent to them. This sort of privacy feature appeals to people who want to share and chat without other people keeping and forwarding their messages.

Snapchat has gained in popularity in recent years. With 187 million daily users, it is in the top 10 social media platforms.[1] Unlike Instagram, many of the filters and lenses for photo editing are sillier and appeal to nonserious photo-takers (Instagram filters often focus on enhancing without being too obvious). Snapchat has taken some criticism for being a place where sexual content, including images, are shared and sometimes unintentionally saved and distributed. Also, the Android version of the Snapchat app has had some bugs that make it less user friendly, but it is something the company is working to improve and change. While that work is in progress, new users may find that Snapchat works better on an iPhone.[2]

WHY DO PEOPLE USE SNAPCHAT?

One of the main reasons people use Snapchat is to communicate and share things, like photos and chats, in a semiprivate environment. The photo, video, and audio filters and lenses on Snapchat are built to be fun and silly. For example, one of the most popular lenses used early on was called the puking rainbow because it edited a selfie to make it look like the person is, you guessed it, puking a rainbow. Other common features include adding dog and cat features to selfies (see figure 5.1), adding background images like cartoon flowers or butterflies, and adding text or unique local images based on where the person is physically located at the time of the photo. Many lenses and filters are only available for a short time. In February 2019, Snapchat offered a Black History Month lens that took users into a virtual gallery featuring black Millennial artists.[3] These options make Snapchat popular with a younger audience but are great for any friends or groups who are keeping in touch about everyday things.

Figure 5.1. Snapchat lenses and filters work on human and even animal faces.

Snapchat is also popular with people who like to be private, or people who feel like there is too much information about them online. Although you can delete posts to other social media sites like Twitter and Facebook, Snapchat is the only sharing platform that deletes by default. For teens and young people who want to joke around and share without their information coming up again later, Snapchat feels safer and easier to maintain. There are still privacy concerns, which are discussed later in this chapter. However, default erasing is a good start for people who don't want a huge backlog of posts out there.

Similarly, people who feel overwhelmed and worry they "just can't catch up" with social media platforms like Facebook and Twitter may like that Snapchat does not offer traditional feeds. You can certainly browse in Snapchat's Discover area to find stories and sponsored reading. But there won't be a never-ending feed of posts from people that keeps getting longer as you scroll down. The trade-off is that Snapchat sometimes has nothing to see if your friends are not that active.

Even those without a Snapchat account can access certain features of Snapchat. For example, anyone can view the Snap Map featuring snaps shared to Our Story. The Snap Map can be reached by going to https://map .snapchat.com on any device, even a desktop computer. The heat map that appears will show where videos have been posted, with red areas being more popular and having more videos (see figure 5.2). This can give you a quick indication of where things are happening in your area, with or without a Snapchat account.

Finally, Snapchat is also popular among people who like selfies and editing images. Snapchat features change often, and stickers and other features can be unique based on your location (note that you must give the app permission to use your location

Figure 5.2. Snapchat's Snap Map shows where recent public videos were created.

CHAPTER 5

to get these features). Location-based filters are called geofilters and usually show some local or location-based pride or flair. For example, when taking a photo in Houston, Texas, you may get a framed image option that shows NASA and a famous Houston mural. Other editing options allow you to cut out part of your photo and use it like a sticker, perhaps adding your sister's face in multiple places in one image. For people who want to play with images and then share them, Snapchat can be a fun tool.

SNAPCHAT TERMINOLOGY

Bitmoji—Bitmoji is a separate app that is often used together with Snapchat. Using Bitmoji you can create cartoon profile images of yourself with a yellow Snapchat-themed frame, suitable for a profile picture on Snapchat. Bitmoji profile pictures are very common on Snapchat.

Emojis—Emojis are tiny image pictures that are typically used in chats and online communication. In Snapchat, some emojis mean specific things when they appear next to your contact names. For example, the flame/fire emoji next to a contact means that you have snapped a person and they have snapped you back every day over multiple days. A birthday cake next to a name means it is that person's birthday. A baby means that you are new friends. There are more than a dozen emojis used this way, and a simple search of "Snapchat emoji" can show the full list to new users.

Filter—A filter is a built-in photo effect on Snapchat that allows you to enhance or change a photo. Many are built specifically for selfies. Filters may add frames, distortion, color changes, or accessories to an image. You can even cut out parts of your image and paste it like a sticker. Some filters are based on location, such as sand and umbrella frames when you are at the beach. You can add filters by swiping left on your image.

Flashback—If you have chosen to save snaps using the Snapchat Memories feature, Snapchat's flashback feature will show up on their yearly anniversaries to remind you what you were doing that day in years past.

Lens—Lenses are animated effects that you can use in Snapchat. They often use facial recognition to detect your face. The lens can add animated hats on your head, butterflies flying above you, or other fun additions. Some lenses can additionally respond to sound. For some events, Snapchat has offered lenses that can be "flipped" to the back camera to see a virtual space.

Memories—Memories is a Snapchat feature that allows users to save a photo or video they have created instead of letting it disappear (the default).

62

Messages—Sending something directly to a friend or a selected group of friends is a message. Friends can view message snaps only twice (one replay is allowed), unlike snaps posted to My Story (which last for 24 hours).

My Story—This is a place to add snaps that all friends can see. Snaps added to your story stay there for 24 hours before disappearing.

Our Story—Like Stories or My Story, Our Story is a collection of snaps. However, Our Story shows snaps from all over Snapchat that share a place, event, or idea. Posting to Our Story is voluntary, and snaps added to it may be visible for longer than 24 hours. To add a snap to Our Story, choose it from the Send To menu, right below My Story.

Selfie—A selfie is a short-range photo that you take of yourself, often with your phone at arm's length.

SnapBack—This is a reply to a snap on Snapchat—when you answer someone's snap with a snap.

Snapcode—Snapcodes work like a follow button when you are with someone live and want to follow them on Snapchat. If someone opens their code in the app, you can point your Snapchat camera at it to start following them on Snapchat.

Snap Map—A Snap Map is a heat map of snaps added to Our Story from a geographic area. You can see the heat map by going to https://map.snapchat.com on any device, even a desktop computer. It will normally adjust to your local area and show you public snaps that have happened recently.

Snaps—Snaps are what you post on Snapchat. These are images you have added and shared.

Stories—Stories are a collection of snaps that can show together. For example, you might have snaps from a fun day together with friends, and the story will show all of the snaps in order to show how great the day was.

THE BASICS OF USING SNAPCHAT

Snapchat is a mobile platform, so you must create an account on your phone or mobile device. You can use a tablet, like an iPad, but the app is built for mobile so it will not have additional features geared toward a larger screen on a tablet. Snapchat asks for your name and date of birth to sign up. Then you must create a unique username and password. Adding a phone number is optional but adding it does allow Snapchat to text you with a reset link if you ever forget your password. Adding an e-mail address is also optional, but you must either add an e-mail address or phone number for account verification.

Once you have created an account, you can adjust your settings in My Profile. You can always get to My Profile by clicking on your profile image at the top of the main screen. My Profile will include your location (if you allow it), your image or Bitmoji, and any trophies you receive (see figure 5.3). You can also see or save stories that you have added to, see and add friends, or change your settings by clicking on the gear icon. If you have added to My Story, you can see the posts you have added there and can click on My Story to see all of the people who have viewed it. Your image/avatar is the main thing that people see from your profile, and you may notice that many people have a similar cartoon-style image of themselves. These images are called Bitmoji, and they are created with a free app with the same name. If you want to create a Bitmoji, you will need to download that app separately. However, once you have it you can link Bitmoji and Snapchat in order to update your cartoon self as often as you like (including outfit changes and facial expressions).

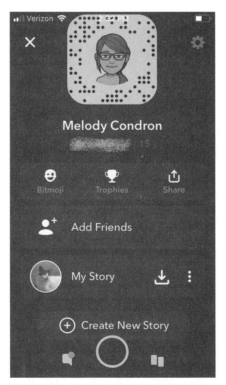

Figure 5.3.   Snapchat's My Profile.

While in My Profile, you can click on the gear icon to change your settings. Under My Account, you will see basic information including your name, username, birthday, contact information, payment information, password maintenance, and connected apps and accounts (such as Bitmoji). There are also purchase options under My Account, including creating your own filters and lenses for events. You can control when Snapchat will send you push notifications in this section as well.

Under the Additional Services heading, you can choose the Manage option to change some of Snapchat's more interesting settings. This menu is where you can turn on and off location-based filters, control the color of your skin in emojis you post, see permissions you have given for your device, and see what Snapchat knows about you for advertising. You can turn off advertising preferences based on audience and activity here. In addition, you can turn on and off "Lifestyle and Interests" options that the app has identified for you. Since you will see advertising in the app either way, you can control what sorts of things you would most like to see from an oddly specific list of groups. For example, you can choose Sharp-Dressed Man, Social Drinkers, and Snow Sports Enthusiasts if you want to see advertising for those target audiences (see figure 5.4). When changing these settings, also keep in mind that it will change what sorts of content you see in the Discover section of Snapchat, including stories and new content suggestions.

Once you have added a profile picture and reviewed your settings, you can play around with the many snap features in the app. Some options on Snapchat seem hidden because you have to swipe to reach them. Others are accessed by clicking on an icon on the screen, which can be confusing if you don't know what the icons mean. In the beginning, when you have not yet connected with friends, click around through

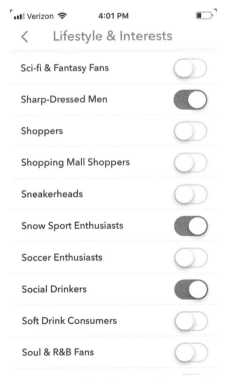

Figure 5.4. Changing your interests in Snapchat's advertising profiles.

the app to practice and play with new features. Many of the basic tools are described here, but many YouTube videos also provide walk-through tutorials for first-time Snapchat users.

The Main / Camera Screen

The main screen is the first thing you see when logging into the Snapchat app (see figure 5.5). This screen is the camera view and is built for taking new snaps and adding filters and lenses. Across the top, you will see your avatar/profile image, a search bar, add friend icon, camera toggle, flash control, and night mode (moon icon). Your profile image will take you to My Profile, where you can adjust settings. Searching in the camera screen bar will help you find friends, public profiles, publisher stories, and other content that matches your keyword. You can also find community lenses and subscription content by searching. Click on the X in the upper right to close out of search and return to the camera screen. Camera toggle allows you to switch between front and back cameras on your phone. Flash control allows you to turn your camera flash on and off without leaving Snapchat. The moon icon lets you switch to night/low light mode when needed.

The large round button at the bottom of the screen is the camera button. You can click it to take a picture or hold it down to take a video. After taking a picture or video, you can edit it with the icons that appear along the right side of the screen. The options (from top to bottom) include T (adding text), Pencil (drawing), Add Stickers, Scissors (cut and paste from your image), Paperclip (include a web link), Crop, and Clock/Timer (see figure 5.6). The timer sets how long the snap will appear to the person you send it to, which can be 1–10 seconds or limitless. Limitless means that the snap will NOT disappear after any amount of time if your friend keeps it open. Once they close and replay it once (which is the limit), it will disappear like any other snap. You can also swipe to the left to see additional filters that will change the image. Clicking on the smiling face to the right of the camera button will give you multiple lens options. Lenses change as you move them around or when they are applied to people's faces. Usually they will give you instructions, such as "Find Face" or "Tap" to see what the lens can do. Once you have selected the lenses and filters you want and have added words and edits, you can save the photo, add it to your story, or send it. Saving to My Story will make the snap available for 24 hours to all of your friends. You can see My Story by clicking on your profile image, where you can save a snap that you did not already save. However, if you send it to a friend and did not save it, you cannot get it back.

Figure 5.5.   Main/camera view in Snap-chat.

Figure 5.6.   Snapchat editing screen options.

Additional icons appear along the bottom of the camera screen. The icon in the center, below the camera button, will take you to your Memories, described later in the chapter. You can also get to Memories by swiping down. Quick access to friends is in the bottom left, and access to Discover is in the bottom right. You can also swipe left or right from the camera screen to get to these features.

Swipe Left for Friends

Swiping left will take you to your friends list. On the friend screen, you can find known contacts by sharing your contact list with Snapchat. You can also search for a friend's username or scan a Snapcode that you have saved from their text to your photos. Note that if your friend is with you in real life, you can just take a snap of their Snapcode from the camera screen to add them to your friend list. Once you connect, you can click on any friend listed to chat and share snaps.

You can also send a snap to someone from the camera screen by choosing send and then picking the friend.

From the friend chat screen, you have multiple options for communicating. You can type into the chat field and send chat messages, which is straightforward and similar to most text messaging. There are also five icons along the bottom of the screen (see figure 5.7):

1. The first icon, which looks like pictures on a phone, lets you choose a photo saved on your phone.
2. The phone icon lets you call your friend through Snapchat.
3. Click on the circle to take a photo or video live, just like on the camera screen. You can also add filters and lenses from this camera view.
4. The video camera icon will video call your friend through Snapchat.
5. The face icon will give you Bitmoji options. When you choose this icon, it brings up additional choices at the bottom, including recently used Bitmoji. If you scroll the options to the left there are additional choices for stickers and other fun additions.

Figure 5.7. Friend screen options.

Swipe Right for Discover

Swiping right from the camera screen brings you to the Discover screen. Your friends' stories will be at the top of the screen if there are any. This is also where you will find any subscriptions you have signed up for. Under the For You option, there will be lots of content, including stories and snaps from publishers and creators that Snapchat thinks you might like. You may also be able to watch an event live: look for the "LIVE" label on stories to watch a live event. Other than your friends and subscriptions, the content in Discover is generated from content you look at, as well as the advertising you have set in Snapchat settings. To see what the app has listed for you, click on your profile image >

Settings > Manage (under Additional Services) > Lifestyle and Interests. You can turn things on and off if you want your advertisements and Discover content to reflect what you like.

Swipe Down for Snap Map

Swiping down will take you to the Snap Map, a heat map based on your current location. The Snap Map shows hot spots where people have recently posted public snaps to Our Story. You can also see stories made up of public snaps that are all from the same event, like a graduation or concert. The Snap Map can also be reached by going to https://map.snapchat.com on any device, even a desktop computer (and even by someone without a Snapchat account). This can give you a quick indication of where things are happening in your area, with or without a Snapchat account. If you post public videos with locations, they may show up on the Snap Map. You will also see yourself (usually as your Bitmoji) on the Snap Map, as well as your friends if they are in the same area.

Swipe Up for Memories

Though Snapchat highlights private sharing, it does offer a Memories feature. Memories captures snaps that you create so that you can save them to your phone's images, look back at them later, edit/filter them later, or even send them to friends long after they were created. Using the function does require a bit of forethought, though. You have to save them before you send them and they disappear. To save to Memories, create a snap like usual. Then, click on the download icon at the bottom of the screen; it looks like an arrow saving to an inbox (see figure 5.8). You can also save an entire story, or just individual snaps from a story. To save a story, go to the Profile button (arrow icon) at the top of the screen and click on the three-dot menu. Click on Story settings, and then the download icon (arrow saving to an inbox) to save.

PRIVACY AND SAFETY

Snapchat presents some unusual privacy and safety issues. The platform prides itself on being more private than many other networks because a lot of its content is not saved. That can create a sense of false security where you feel like it is safe to post private photos or information on Snapchat, which can be dangerous. Though the app will let you know if someone takes a screen capture of your snap,

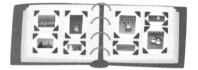

Welcome to Memories!

Memories is a personal collection of
the Snaps and Stories you save,
backed up by Snapchat.

learn more

Okay

Figure 5.8. Saving a snap to Memories.

there are multiple third-party apps that allow you to log in to Snapchat and save a snap without alerting the person who posted it. It is also common for someone to take a photo of a phone's screen with another phone or camera. If that happens, the sender will not know that the snap has been saved. Also, though an image may disappear from your feed that does not mean it has been deleted everywhere. As with any online tool, it is important to follow general common sense even when things are supposed to be private: don't post anything on social media that you do not want to be public or shared with people other than the receiver.

Another thing to keep in mind is whether you want to give the Snapchat application access to your photos, microphone, contacts, and location. Some of the app's features, including geofilters, are only available if you give permission to location, and the other permissions will allow you to do basic things like find your friends. However, as with any app, the more access you allow, the greater risk there is if there is ever a data breach at Snapchat or one of its partner companies. Access to your device and data are all controlled in Settings (the gear icon accessed in My Profile) under the Additional Services heading. Click Manage >

Permissions to see what is enabled. To turn these off, you may have to go to the settings on your specific device.

There are multiple ways to limit Snapchat access to your location. In the Who Can section on location, you can make adjustments, including selecting specific friends who can see where you are in real time. You can also set it to all friends, or all friends except specific people. In addition, you can also go into Ghost Mode by toggling on the available ghost button. When in Ghost Mode, no one can see your location (but Snapchat still knows where you are). Also in the Manage menu, you can click on Maps to allow or deny anonymized use of your location data with the Snapchat map providers. Farther down in settings, you can clear the top locations in your account, resetting any location information that Snapchat keeps on you. To truly deny the app access, you must go to your device's settings and either turn off location services completely or turn them off for just the Snapchat app. On an iPhone, that function is found in Settings > Privacy. On an Android device, go to Settings > Apps and Notifications > App Permissions. If location access concerns you, you can always turn it off and on as needed. Keep in mind that many features, including most filters and lenses, will not work without location access turned on.

Some Safety Tips for Snapchat

- When looking through settings, check all of the options under the Who Can header. These include controls for who can view your story, contact you, and see your location.
- If you do not want people to know your birthday, the Birthday Party feature that adds a cake next to your name can be turned off in user settings (click on your avatar then the gear icon to go to your settings).
- Snapchat offers account verification, which means that you can verify your account via text message. If someone tries to log in to your account and does not have access to your phone, then this will prevent unauthorized access.
- If you want to avoid your account coming up in the Quick Add section of Snapchat (where the app suggests people to follow to other users), then you can turn that feature off. Click on your avatar and then the settings gear icon, then scroll to the See Me in Quick Add menu option to make the change.
- If you do not like the idea of Snapchat and advertisers tracking you across multiple platforms, go to Settings > Manage > Ad Preferences and turn Audience-Based and Activity-Based ads off. You will still see advertising,

but it will not be based on your searches outside of Snapchat. That means you may see more ads that do not appeal to you, but it also reduces the information about you that is shared between companies.

- If you ever see a snap you want to report to Snapchat, you can tap the up arrow icon to report it.

SPECIAL FEATURES IN SNAPCHAT

Flashback Memories is a Snapchat function that sends you saved snaps from the past in your memories. It only works if you save snaps, and the app sends the memories on the anniversary day of when the snap was taken. When it shows up in Memories, the snap can be shared with friends or saved on the camera roll. If you would rather not have these flashback memories, the function can be turned off in settings (gear icon) by clicking on Memories > Features and un-toggling the Flashback button. The Flashback feature won't work if you never save anything to Memories.

Shake to Report is a weird way to communicate directly with Snapchat to suggest improvements or report technical issues. By turning the function on, you can literally shake your device, and a menu will pop up. You can report a problem or suggest improvements and click Submit. If you like this function, you can even change how sensitive the shake response is so that it does not go off every time you move around. You can turn Shake to Report on in settings (click on your image then the gear icon) by clicking on Shake to Report.

Creating your own geofilter in Snapchat is now possible, for a fee. The Geo-Filter feature is used to create custom filters and lenses for weddings, parties, and other group events. The cost depends on the size of the geographic area where the geofilter will be used, as well as the amount of time it will be available. There are instructions and video tutorials online, but the process to create your own filter is pretty easy. In your account, click on your avatar and then Settings (the gear icon). Click on Filters and Lenses. Snapchat will make themed suggestions based on what sort of occasion you are planning for, including appropriate text, frames, and more. Geofilters start at around $5.99 and get more expensive based on the size and time available.

INSTAGRAM

Instagram is a photo- and video-sharing platform that has quickly become one of the most popular social media options in the United States and abroad. The platform is built for mobile use, such as a phone or tablet. Accounts and photos can be viewed in a computer browser, but some functionality is limited to mobile. For example, users can only post from the mobile app. Instagram is owned by Facebook but has a very different approach to networking and sharing. While some accounts are private and limited to just friends and family, as is common with Facebook, there are a lot more public-facing Instagram accounts.

WHY DO PEOPLE USE INSTAGRAM?

Instagram was created for photo sharing from mobile devices. Having a camera in every phone has made digital photos available immediately, and many people want to share things while they are in the moment. Many Instagram users post photos right after they take them in order to share their life experiences and day-to-day happenings with friends and family. Because it is photo and video focused, users cannot add a text-only post. The use of images more than text makes Instagram a fast way to keep in touch and see things that are happening. Users choose their best or favorite photos and can add filters to highlight or change the photos. This can result in fun and interesting posts.

An Instagram account does not need to have the photos all fit into one category. However, some Instagram users (individuals as well as organizations) have a themed page, such as all photos of animals or Lego buildings. Nonprofits and churches often post photos from events that they plan. Foodies might have an account only of food and restaurant photos. However, quite a few people post photos on a variety of subjects as they go through their day. It may be helpful to list the kinds of photos you plan to post in your profile bio so that others will know whether they want to follow you.

Instagram has also become so popular that people are creating ways to use it in real-life scenarios beyond everyday posting. Real estate agents posting homes for sale may encourage people to post photos from open houses.[1] 29Rooms in Los Angeles has dubbed itself an "Instagram Museum," with spaces and backdrops specifically made for posting selfies.[2] Wedding planners and couples are also designating hashtags encouraging their invited guests to post their best wedding photos to Instagram.[3] Overall, Instagram is a popular place to interact with the world through pictures.

INSTAGRAM TERMINOLOGY

Bio—The bio in your Instagram profile is where you can describe yourself, your account, and/or your posts. A hashtag or handle listed in your bio will become linked to that hashtag search or account. There is no right or wrong thing to have in a bio. Some users have poetry or a famous quote. Others list what sorts of photos they plan to post. You can change your bio as often as you like.

Caption—Photos and videos are the main part of a post, and captions can be used to describe what appears or to add hashtags for related topics.

Collection—Users can add photos to a saved collection by clicking on the bookmark icon below the post. Once photos are saved, they can be accessed by clicking on the triple-bar icon in the upper right of the profile screen and selecting the Saved menu option.

Comment—Users can comment on posts by clicking on the word bubble icon under the post. To add the comment, click into the Add a Comment box and then click Post. Emojis are also available above the comment box. If you add someone's handle (@username) in a comment, they will get a notification about the post, and many people do this to share a post with others. You can also add hashtags. Sometimes the author of the post adds additional hashtags in a comment if they forgot to add them to the original caption.

Direct Message (DM)—Instagram users can contact one another directly in a nonpublic chat using the Direct Message feature. To send a direct message, click on the arrow icon in the upper right of the mobile screen and search for the user you want to message.

Double Tap/ Heart / Like—When users like a post on Instagram, they can double tap the heart icon on the post, and the user who posted the photo will get a notification. The author of the post can see how many likes a post has received underneath the post.

Feed / Home—The main screen that Instagrammers see when they log in is called the home screen; it is also called the user's feed. This is where posts from all the people that they follow will appear.

Filter – Instagram features many filters that can change and highlight images and videos that users post to the site. Users will see the filter options when they are creating a post. Sometimes users use the hashtag #nofilter when they are posting a photo or video that is visually amazing without a filter.

Follow/Follower—Instagram users can follow other accounts. Once you follow someone, you will see their posts on your home screen or feed. Users do not need to follow everyone who follows them. Anyone can follow a public account, whether or not they know that person. Users who want to limit who can follow their posts should create a private account.

Handle / IG Handle—As with Twitter, a user's handle is their unique username, starting with an @ symbol. So, IG Handle refers to an Instagram username. Users can mention one another on Instagram by putting a user's handle in a caption.

Hashtag—A hashtag is a keyword or phrase without spaces that starts with a hash/number [#] symbol in front of it. Hashtags help people find posts and photos on the same topic. Hashtags are used heavily on Instagram, and often the caption for a post will only contain hashtags (see figure 6.1). On Instagram, hashtags are linked so users can click through to see more photos that use that hashtag. Users can also search for a hashtag to find related posts. Instagram posts do not have to use hashtags.

IG / IGers—These terms are short for Instagram and Instagrammers and are slang for people who are on Instagram.

Influencers—An Instagram influencer is a person who has built up a large following on the platform. Famous people may be influencers, and other influencers are people who have become well known on Instagram for their posts. Often influencers are paid to promote products in their photos or to use certain hashtags. This is an indirect form of advertising that is common on Instagram.

Instagram Live—Instagram Live is an option for users to live stream what they are doing on video. While streaming, an announcement goes out to the

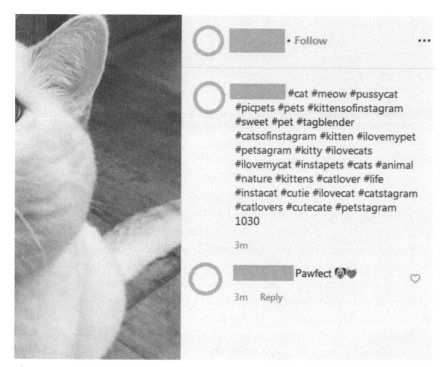

Figure 6.1. Instagram posts often use a lot of hashtags.

user's followers that they are live. Live streams can be saved to Instagram Stories, where they can stay available for 24 hours after the live event.

Instagram Stories—Instagram Stories lets users post photos and video that disappear after 24 hours. Like functionality on the social media platform Snapchat, users create content that is not meant to be kept forever.

Latergram / #Latergram—This is a term used for posts that are added to Instagram after they are taken, often days or weeks later. Usually this is indicated by adding the hashtag #latergram in a caption. This tells people that the photo or video they are viewing is not real time. This is not required but can help with confusion for those who often use Instagram in real time.

Post—Uploading a photo and any related captions is called a post on Instagram. Instagram is media focused, so posts must include media such as a photo or video.

Tag or Mention—Instagram users can mention or tag another user by mentioning that user's handle in a post. This is common if the photo has another user in it, but it can also be used if you want that user to see the post.

THE BASICS OF USING INSTAGRAM

New users can create an Instagram account by downloading the app from the iPhone App Store or the Android Google Play Store, depending on which device they own. The app can be installed on multiple devices even if they are not using the same operating system, and users will still be able to log in to their account. For example, a user with an Android phone and an iPad tablet will be able to get both apps and log in to the same user account. Once the app is downloaded, you can click on the app and choose Create New Account. You will need to provide either a phone number or an e-mail address. You can also choose to log in using your Facebook account (Instagram is owned by Facebook). Depending on your account choices, you may need to check your text messages or e-mail for a confirmation code from Instagram. This is how they check to make sure the phone number or e-mail that you provided are correct. You can also create an account using a desktop or laptop computer by going to instagram.com. Users must then create a username. Usernames are unique on Instagram, and the username you want to use may not be available. Instagram will suggest similar names if the username you want has been taken. It is common to add numbers or underscore [_] to a chosen name to make it unique. Keep in mind that names that are confusing or close to too many other names may make it easy for people to mistake you for other users.

Figures 6.2 and 6.3 show Instagram's main screens on a mobile and desktop. There are more features on the mobile screen (figure 6.2) than there are on the desktop screen (figure 6.3). However, some features on the non-mobile site are not available in the app, including temporarily disabling and deleting an account.

The main options available in Instagram appear at the bottom of the mobile screen shown in figure 6.2. The house icon will return users to the home screen, which shows their personalized feed of posts from their followers. The other icons along the bottom are search and explore (magnifying glass icon), create a new post (plus sign icon), notifications (heart icon), and bio and account (person icon). The camera icon in the upper left is for Instagram Live and Instagram Stories, explained later in the chapter. The arrow icon in the upper right takes users to their direct messages.

Search and Browse

To search in Instagram, you can click on the icon that looks like a magnifying glass. The Magnifying Glass menu option helps users explore posts and news beyond their followers (see figure 6.4). There is a search bar at the top where

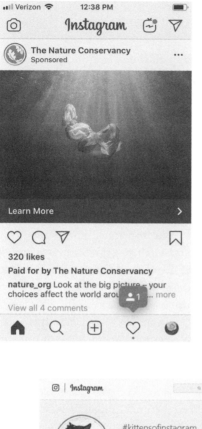

Figure 6.2.   View of Instagram mobile.

Figure 6.3.   View of Instagram from a computer.

Figure 6.4. Explore new things using the magnifying glass icon.

users can search for specific hashtags and usernames, or for subjects and keywords. Once you search, you can limit results to people, tags, places, or the top posts (based on likes and comments). The Explore area is often populated with posts and suggestions similar to those the user already follows. So, for example, if you follow lots of beauty and hairstyle Instagram accounts, you may see suggestions for those topics in the Explore area.

How to Post

To post on Instagram, choose the plus sign icon along the bottom and choose a photograph or video from your device. The last photo taken on the device may appear in the main part of the screen. Additional photos from your device will appear below. The photos you took most recently will be at the top of your camera roll, but you can scroll through to find older photos, or you can use the drop-down option at the top to look at your favorites or other lists. If you would like to put multiple photos in one post, you can do that by clicking on the icon that looks like stacked pages. It will appear in the lower right-hand corner of the photo.

Once you have selected a photo, photos, or video to post, click Next. Instagram provides dozens of filters to modify photos and videos. Filters can make colors more vibrant, change images to black and white or sepia tone, and adjust colors. Clicking on each filter will show you what the photo will look like using that filter so you can see the options before the item is posted. Clicking Edit at the bottom of the screen will show other adjustment options, including contrast, brightness, sharpness, and more. Any changes will be saved as a new photo or video, so the original will not be changed. Both will show up in the phone's photos after the post. After clicking Next again, the final screen has options for adding a caption (which often includes hashtags), tagging people, and adding a location. After adding this information and clicking Share, the post will be posted to Instagram for others to see.

Notifications

Instagram users can see notifications for their account and the accounts they follow by clicking on the heart icon at the bottom of the screen. By choosing the Following button at the top, updates on followed accounts will show up, including posts and likes. By choosing the You button at the top of the screen, users can see their own notifications. This will include a chronological timeline of your activity and activity around your posts. For example, it will include likes that your posts have received as well as posts you liked. It will also tell you when someone new starts to follow you if anyone tags you by using your username in a post or comment. Interactions with other users will also include a Follow button if you do not currently follow that user (if you already follow that user, it will say Following).

Bio and Profile

The bio and profile page can be accessed by clicking on the small person icon in the lower right of the app screen. This screen will show users their own account, including their profile picture, bio, number of followers, and all of their posts. Users can click on their followers or the number of people they are following to see a list of those Instagram users. They can edit who they follow on that list. While viewing the profile and bio, you can click on Edit Profile to change the name, username, website, bio statement, and other profile information. You can also change the profile photo.

PRIVACY AND SAFETY

By default, Instagram accounts and posts are public. Public accounts are obviously a larger privacy concern than private accounts, where you can choose who can follow you. Photos of yourself, your children and family, or the inside of your home are all things that you may not want to be posted publicly. If you do want to have a private account, you can change your account by going to your profile and clicking on the triple-bar menu (sometimes called the hamburger). Then, click on Settings > Account Privacy and toggle the button to turn Private Account on (see figure 6.5). Once you turn on the Private Account option you will need to approve all follow requests in order for other people to see your posts, even if they followed you beforehand. Requests will appear in the Activity list, which looks like a heart on the main page.

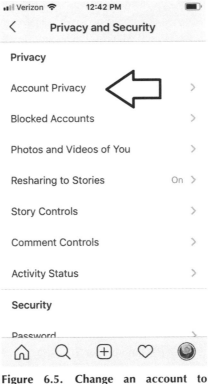

Figure 6.5. Change an account to private.

Controlling location options is something all users with public Instagram accounts should do consciously. Photo location details are not retained from the original photo, so posting a photo will not automatically share the location. However, when a photo is first posted the app will access the location data and will suggest a location to tag. Very often you have options to choose a very specific location, which may be fine for public places. If you are at your own or another person's home, using a neighborhood name is not recommended. Instead, choose the city name or no location at all. If you have set the location on previous posts and you want to remove those locations, you can. In the post, click on the location name and choose Remove Location.

Additional options for increasing or controlling privacy and security can be found by clicking on Settings and scrolling down to Privacy and Security. Here, there are individual menus to help you control many things, including your activity status (this shows when you are active on the site); who can see your Instagram Stories; who can comment on your posts; hiding offensive comments; two-factor authentication; and more. The Privacy and Security Help menu option is a good place to start if you want to review your settings or are just getting started with Instagram.

Users can block accounts of other Instagram users who are harassing or otherwise bothering them. To block another user, tap on their username to go to their user profile page. Click on the triple-dot icon at the top of the screen and choose Block.

HELP AND SPECIAL FEATURES

Instagram Settings can be difficult to find because they are all nested in a mobile app, but there is a lot of hidden functionality. To see all Settings, go to your profile screen (the icon looks like a person) and click on the triple-bar at the top of the screen and choose Settings from the bottom of the menu that appears. There are dozens of menu options to choose from inside Settings. Some examples include see how much time you spend on the app (under Your Activity), review posts you've liked (under Account), and pause all notifications from Instagram with one button (under Notifications).

Third-party integration is common for Instagram. Instagram is integrated with many other social sites, and several third-party apps exist to add to the Instagram experience. Most notably, users can choose to link their Facebook, Twitter, or Tumblr accounts. Linking accounts lets users choose whether they want a photo to show up on additional sites at the same time that they post to Instagram.

Instagram Stories and *Instagram Live* are features that allow for more interaction between Instagram users. Instagram Stories lets users post photos and video that disappear after 24 hours. Instagram Live allows users to post a live stream video of themselves. Both features can be accessed by clicking on the camera icon in the upper right corner of the app and selecting either Instagram Live or Create Instagram Story. There is an opportunity to add options, such as hiding a story from a certain person or people or making it only available to your followers. You can even make videos only available to people who you follow who follow you back. Even though Stories will disappear from Instagram after 24 hours, you also have the option to save them to your phone so they are not truly lost forever—they are just no longer on the site. Using Instagram Stories and Live can engage the people who follow you in a different way. For example, if you post exciting or interesting things they will want to check your posts often to not miss a story before it is deleted. Obviously, this applies more to people who are using Instagram for promotion of something like a business or event.

Instagram Help Center can be reached by going to your profile screen (the icon looks like a little person) and clicking on the triple-bar menu in the upper right, clicking on Settings, and scrolling to Help Center. By selecting Help Center, users get to a list of options but also an open search so that they can ask a specific question. The Help Center is the best place to start if you cannot find a setting or option. It also contains helpful information for Instagram users, including a Tips for Parents page and site Privacy Terms.

Deleting your account on Instagram can be challenging. While you can set up an account using the app and a mobile device, you can only delete an account using the website version of Instagram on a computer or laptop.[4] If you do not remember your password because you saved it in the app, this can be difficult, and you may have to reset account access to create a new password. Once you are able to log in to your Instagram account using a browser, you can search for the Delete Your Account page in the Instagram Help Center at http://help.instagram.com. You will have to choose why you are deleting the account from a drop-down list. Once you have selected an answer, you can click Permanently Delete My Account. All posts, comments, videos, likes, and followers will be deleted. You can also temporarily disable your account, which will not delete everything. Using a browser (not the app), log in to your account, choose the person icon in the top right, and select Edit Profile. Temporarily Disable My Account is available as an option at the bottom. You will need to provide your password and say why you want to disable the account in order to use this function.

REDDIT

Reddit is a social news site where users create, discuss, and rate content. Members add content like links, images, and news, and other members vote items up or down. Items that are voted up appear higher in the feed, so that the most popular and interesting items rise to the top for others to view. Subject-focused communities called subreddits each focus on a different topic, and users of the site can choose which subreddits they want to add to and follow. Reddit launched in 2005 to immediate popularity and continues to be popular. It is sometimes called "the front page of the internet" because it can seem like the starting point for many issues and news items that later become memes and mainstream stories.[1] It is the fourth most popular social media site for Americans, with more than 300 million monthly users.[2] However, it can also be chaotic and overwhelming. As Brett Molina states in his article in *USA Today*, "There is perhaps no other site on the Internet more informative, entertaining, and confusing to use than Reddit."[3]

WHY DO PEOPLE USE REDDIT?

Like Twitter, many people use Reddit because it is an unfiltered and up-to-the-minute collection of posts. People who use Reddit may post to the site about a newsworthy event long before official news agencies catch up.[4] Brett Molina again explains, "Nearly everything you have seen catching viral buzz online likely started on Reddit."[5] Beyond news, Reddit has discussions about virtually any and every topic, from basic things like sports, animals, and travel, to more obscure things like short stories with no point and an entire community posting photos of wolves eating watermelon. There is literally something for everyone on the massive, active platform. This makes it great for chatting about topics of interest or just browsing for new ideas and random information.

Some Reddit members are there primarily for entertainment. Subreddit communities like /r/gifs (a community that posts short animated videos on any topic) are an easy way to waste time and see new things on a variety of subjects. The same is true of the subreddit /r/jokes, which is just 100 percent jokes. Because you can choose which communities to follow, Reddit can be a place to get away from news and politics. Occasionally items unrelated to a subreddit community are posted there, but they are quickly voted down by the community members. This self-regulation usually means that Reddit members will primarily see things that fit into the communities they have chosen. This is unlike some other social media sites, where you follow specific people and then see all of their posts, regardless of the subject matter.

People who are interested in niche topics or who have a silly sense of humor will likely find a home on Reddit. You can easily search for any topic using the search bar in the upper-right corner. Hobbies, interests, and news topics will all be covered by a subreddit, as will stranger topics. Here are a few of the strange subreddits available on the platform:

- /r/birdswitharms is an entire community posting and discussing photo-shopped pictures of birds with arms.
- /r/lifeofnorman is a subreddit of people directing the actions of a fictional, unremarkable man named Norman.
- /r/pointless is a place for people to tell pointless stories.
- /r/Mirrorsforsale is an entire page of people posting photos of mirrors for sale.

Reddit members can follow along to see what is posted and vote things up and down, even if they do not add their own posts and content. So, if you don't have a mirror to sell, you can still participate in /r/Mirrorsforsale.

While there are hundreds of silly and weird subreddits, there are also many more serious discussions on news and helpful topics. Some popular subreddits include the following:

- /r/lifehacks is a community of people sharing ideas for simplifying their lives.

- /r/texas is for Texas news, but almost every state and location has its own thread.
- /r/IAMA is the Reddit Ask Me Anything page, where famous people and others with interesting experiences open the floor to questions about anything.
- /r/GetMotivated is full of people sharing inspiring and motivating ideas.

These and other communities allow people to get what they want from the internet in a more focused way than searching Google. If the community does not exist, any member with an account can create it.

Because it has communities for everything, Reddit can also be a place to discuss controversial topics. Reddit members do not have to verify their e-mail accounts or add much detail to their profile, making them somewhat anonymous. Anonymity makes it possible to ask questions and make comments without as much concern for repercussions. Reddit has gotten a negative spotlight on more than one occasion for subreddits focused on controversial topics, including violence toward women and pornography.[6] In 2018, the platform began removing explicit content from their main public page, though explicit sexual and violent content is still very much available on the site.[7] Reddit CEO Yishan Wong has defended this, saying, "We stand for free speech. This means we are not going to ban distasteful subreddits. We will not ban legal content even if we find it odious or if we personally condemn it."[8] This means that people who do not want to view this content must be cautious of which subreddits they follow and what they view when and if they choose to use Reddit. Those users can also reduce the number of adult or offensive posts in their feed by turning off adult content (which is off by default) in User Settings.

REDDIT TERMINOLOGY

Subreddit—A subreddit is a community on Reddit devoted to a certain topic. Subreddits have names that correlate with their address on the Reddit site and always start with /r/. For example, /r/soccer is the Reddit discussion board for soccer. There are also many, more specific subreddits devoted to soccer, and new subreddits appear all the time to fill the needs of those on the platform.

Front Page—This is the main page of Reddit where you will see the most popular and currently trending topics being discussed.

Home Page—This is a Reddit member's personalized list of posts from subreddit communities that they have chosen to follow.

Troll—*Troll* is a term used that is not limited to Reddit but is commonly used on the site. It is a term used to describe a person who posts controversial or upsetting content in order to get a response from other people. Sometimes people will post something to a subreddit that is not on topic. Instead of commenting or engaging that person, it is best to just downvote the post.

Moderator—Moderators are volunteers who manage a specific subreddit. They enforce the rules of the subreddit and may remove unrelated content, ban problematic users, or keep the subreddit on topic.

Admin—Reddit Admins work for the social media platform. They can manage volunteer moderator capabilities and manage subreddits that may be problematic.

Upvote / Downvote—Every Reddit post has up and down arrows next to it. Other members can use the arrows to vote a post up or down. Votes up mean the post is good, and it will get higher on the list so that more people will see it. Votes down will result in the post being lower on the list. Most of the time, upvoting helps the best things rise to the top. Downvoting is especially helpful when a post is off topic or unhelpful.

Karma—Karma is a reward earned on Reddit by contributing links and comments. If your comments are downvoted below zero then you will lose karma. Some subreddits require good karma to reach them, and higher karma is an indication that people are popular and active on the site.

OP—On Reddit, OP stands for Original Post. This means that the person posting claims to be the creator of the post. This is often used for images and videos.

AMA—AMA stands for Ask Me Anything. Ask Me Anything posts became popular early on Reddit and continue to be a big draw on the platform. It is often used when a famous person or someone who had an interesting experience creates a subreddit to answer questions from the community.

Trophies—Reddit uses gamification as part of membership. Trophies are basically awards that appear in a user's account for achieving certain milestones on Reddit. For example, users who verify their e-mail will get a Verified Email trophy that appears in their account "trophy case." A list of trophies can be found at reddit.com/wiki/trophies.

Reddit Gold—This is the paid, upgraded version of Reddit. Gold members have access to a few additional subreddits and tools, and they may get to test and use new features.

NSFW—This is an acronym that means "not safe for work." It may be used to indicate images, content, or humor that would not be appropriate to look at while in the workplace.

THE BASICS OF USING REDDIT

Reddit can be used on a computer, phone, or other mobile device. Anyone can browse on Reddit without an account. However, people must register as members in order to post, comment, and vote. Creating an account is very easy, and verification via e-mail is not required. Once you are a member, you can subscribe to subreddits that you want to follow, gain karma, and start your own subreddit discussions. Unlike Facebook, Twitter, and many other networks, Reddit is focused more on the content than the people. User profiles are sometimes very basic and have little or no personal information. Real names are rarely used. To adjust profile information, users can click on the drop-down menu in the upper right, next to their profile image (in a browser) or click on the profile image in the upper left (in the app). Choose My Profile > Edit to change your profile image, display name, and About information.

Logged-in members can save settings, including viewing and sorting settings. Controlling these options can sometimes help new users make sense of the massive number of posts on the Reddit /r/All page. In a computer browser, users can choose how compact things appear on their screen by using the view options: Card for larger icons and more space; Classic for medium spacing; and Compact for compressed, tight spacing between stories and posts. Posts can also be sorted by Best, Hot, New, Controversial, Top, and Rising (shown in figure 7.1). Mobile users have the same options for sorting posts and can browse by choosing News, Home, and Popular from the top of the screen. They can also choose card, classic, and media gallery views by clicking on the horizontal bar icons. Media gallery allows mobile users to see media like images and videos in an easier layout for mobile.

New members will want to search for topics they like in the search bar or browse /r/All (the main page) to see the most popular topics of the moment. Once you find subreddits that you like, you can click on them to go to the subreddit community. Click Subscribe if you would like to follow the subreddit and have posts from that community show up in your home feed. You can also follow a specific user by clicking on their username in the post. Look for the username at the top of the post next to the user's profile image and the name of the subreddit. It should say "posted by u/username," which is linked to that user's profile page. Keep in mind that users may comment and post on a wide variety of subjects, so following a user is often less consistent than subscribing to a subject-focused subreddit.

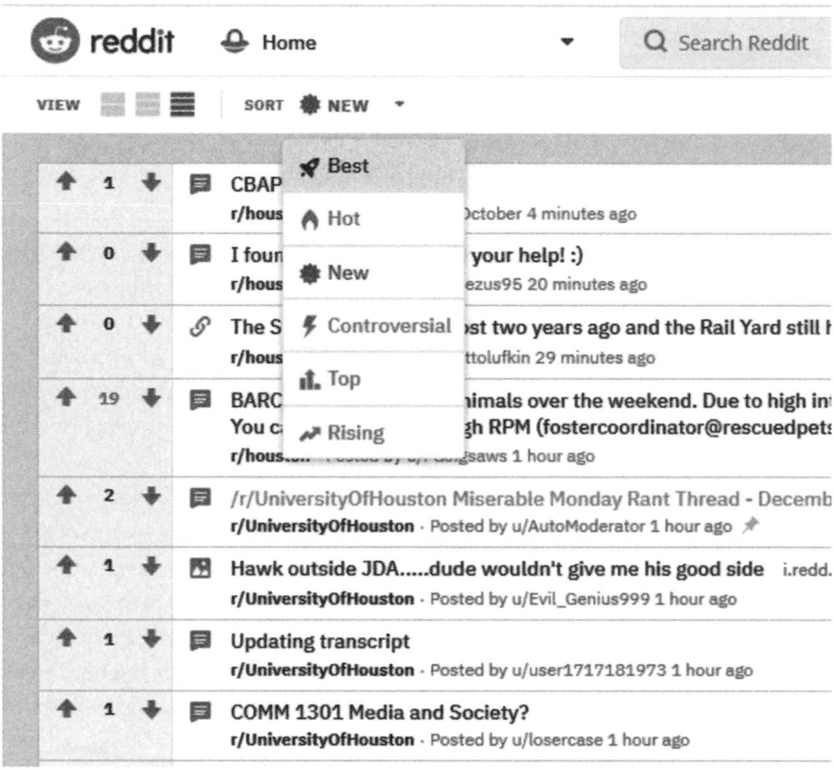

Figure 7.1. Best, Hot, New, and other popular posts on Reddit/r/All.

Once new members choose subreddits and users to follow, their main screen after logging in will default to their home screen. Home will show all the latest items posted from those subreddits and users. Viewing the home screen is helpful if you have a few things you want to keep up with but do not want to delve too deeply into other topics.

Clicking on the drop-down menu at the top of the screen, Reddit members can navigate to other areas on the site (shown in figure 7.2). Users can always return to their home screen by choosing the Home navigation. They can also go to the Popular feed to see the most popular items of the moment or all Reddit posts together. You can also choose OC (original content) to see posts that are reported to be created by the person posting on Reddit. Because it is supposed to be original, the OC area is a place to see new posts you won't find anywhere else . . . at least until they get picked up and become popular across the internet.

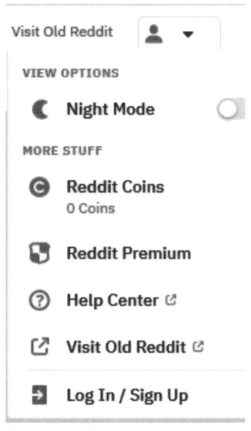

Figure 7.2.   Reddit drop-down menu.

Once you have established an account and start posting, you can review your activity by navigating to My Profile. You can do that by clicking on your user profile image and choosing My Profile. You can also navigate to your profile, or another user's profile, by typing in reddit.com/user/ and your username at the end. For example, you can type in reddit.com/user/Ninja to get to the user profile for the Reddit member with the username Ninja. In the user profile, you can choose to see posts, comments, or an overview of all activity.

Once you have an account and follow subreddits, it is likely that you will find an opportunity to share your own comments or posts. Before posting in a subreddit, be sure to read the community's rules. Rules can be found in the sidebar of the subreddit (in a browser) or by clicking About (in the app). Each subreddit can make its own rules, and sometimes they are strange. For example,

/r/totallynotrobots requires users to not ask for upvotes, use all caps, and always tag NSFW posts. Users may want to browse and read posts in their chosen subreddits before they post themselves so they know their post will be on topic. Reddit also suggests some general rules for posting, including looking for the original source for content and checking for duplicate posts (see figure 7.3).

To add your post, click on the pencil icon at the bottom (in the app), or click Create Post from the sidebar if you are viewing the subreddit on a computer. You can choose whether you will add a text post, image and video, or link. There are basic text-editing options, as well as options to mark the post with special notices of *Spoiler*, *NSFW* (Not Safe for Work), or *OC* (Original Content). Replying and commenting on existing posts is even easier. In the subreddit, you can click on any post to see the comment box. Add your comment and click Comment to submit. Both posts and comments can be upvoted or downvoted. If you see a post in one subreddit that also fits another, you can click Share (or click the arrow icon) to copy a link to the post or to cross-post to another subreddit.

Figure 7.3.   General Reddit rules.

PRIVACY AND SAFETY

Being private and safe on Reddit can be challenging. It is a public network so, like Twitter, anything that you share can be saved and accessed by anyone (even if they do not have a Reddit account). However, Reddit also does not require real names or even an e-mail address to sign up. That means that you can be relatively anonymous if you choose to be. Upvoting and downvoting items does not draw much attention, and occasional posts with limited personal information will make it difficult for anyone to know who you are.

Do keep in mind, though, that Reddit is not completely anonymous, although it may feel that way. The site tracks IP addresses, and police and government entities have access to the site and all content posted there. Police and government interest is mainly to identify illegal behavior, so avoiding posts and subreddits about such behavior is advisable. Other Reddit users may also be able to glean information from a person's account and identify them in real life. Since posts are public and can be viewed by anyone, even without an account, it is safest to limit how much personal information you share on Reddit. You can also limit whether your posts appear in the wide-reaching /r/all feed by clicking on the profile image > My Profile > Edit. There you can choose whether your posts can appear in the larger /r/all list. You can also change whether the subreddits you follow will appear as a list when someone looks at your profile screen.

You should also be conscious of who you interact with directly on the site. Occasionally on Reddit you may come across trolls—people who will post comments, responses, or images just to be disruptive or to get a negative reaction from other Reddit members. Rather than engage these people or tell them they should stop, Reddit users can just vote down their posts and comments. Engaging them often encourages them to post more and may even result in direct messages from them. Users can control who they receive direct messages from on Reddit. By clicking on their user profile image in the upper left (in the app) or upper right (in a browser), users can choose User Settings, then Privacy and Security to control their direct messaging preferences.

Thankfully, some safety features are built in. Like many social media sites, Reddit removed EXIF metadata in photos, including location information. So, photos shared on the site will not have geographic location data like longitude and latitude. Remember, however, that photos can be tracked in other ways. Since posts are public, users may not want to post photos taken in front of their home or in front of a recognizable place that they visit often. While this may seem overly cautious to some users, women in particular may feel safer if they know that their location is not easy to track in photos that they post on the site.

Some Safety Tips for Reddit

- If you want to use Reddit anonymously, avoid posting comments and photos that will make it easier for people to identify you. For example, do not share where you work or what kind of job you have.
- Turn off the option to show your active communities on your profile page. Since many people follow subreddits on topics related to their local area, their work, and their hobbies, seeing them all listed together may make it easy for others to identify you. You can turn off this option in My Profile > Edit Profile.
- If you want to be anonymous while still being logged in to Reddit, click on the user profile image and choose the drop-down menu next to the username. You can choose your username or anonymous.
- Reddit users can choose whether they want to have direct messages from any other users or just trusted users that they have designated. Change "Who can message you" to "Whitelisted" so that you only get direct messages from people you have approved. You can make this change by clicking on your profile image > User Settings > Privacy and Security.
- Do not connect your Twitter profile to your Reddit profile (an option available in User Settings) unless you are okay with less anonymity or are limiting what personal information you post on both sites.
- Limit how many other apps you link to Reddit. Data breaches are common, and the fewer places that have your login information, the safer your account will be.

SPECIAL FEATURES AND HELP

Reddit Traffic tool is an interesting feature on Reddit for users who create their own subreddits. Traffic will show statistics for subreddits that you have created, including pageviews, traffic, and subscriptions. To use it, click on your user profile image and go to My Profile. Choose More Options and then Profile Moderation to get to some of the subreddit moderation tools. There are several charts and other visuals to show the popularity and interaction on your subreddits.

Redditgifts is a real-world gift exchange between Reddit members that happens periodically for holidays and events. It works a lot like the common gift exchange Secret Santa. Users sign up with their e-mail and get matched to other users. They then pick out a gift, mail it, and then confirm online that it was mailed. When your gift arrives from the other user, you are expected to post photos to Reddit. To view Redditgifts, users can click on Redditgifts from the corporate menu in the bottom right of the screen when viewing in a browser, or they can navigate to redditgifts.com, or sometimes randomly with or without a theme. For example, the Kitchen Goods 2018 gift exchange coordinated a gift swap of kitchen items for 1,585 members. More than 100,000 participants sign up for holiday exchanges. Past exchanges can all be viewed online with participating statistics and photos of received gifts (see figure 7.4)

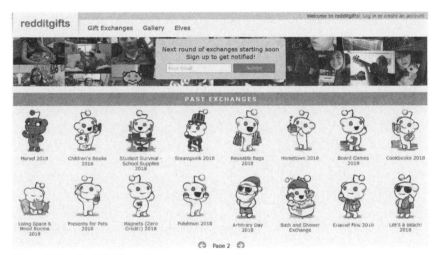

Figure 7.4.   Redditgift exchanges.

LINKEDIN

LinkedIn is a social media platform used for professional networking, including job hunting and keeping up with the professional highlights of current and former business relations. The platform calls itself the world's largest professional network, boasting "more than 562 million users in more than 200 countries worldwide."[1] Many of the features on the site are free, and users can create profiles for themselves that list their experience, skills, and education. In addition, LinkedIn users can connect to other people, follow specific companies or organizations, and follow news put out by leaders in an organization and field. More active members may use the platform to regularly share news about projects and/or updates about their work. The platform is available on the web through a browser (see figure 8.1) or using the LinkedIn mobile application. LinkedIn also offers other mobile apps for more specific purposes, including LinkedIn Job Search and LinkedIn Slide Share.

Businesses are very involved on LinkedIn, and people may be encouraged by their workplace to keep a LinkedIn account current.[2] Some workplaces may consider use of LinkedIn a work activity, since it can reflect well on the organization if their employees are engaged professionally. Whether or not a workplace promotes its use, LinkedIn is also a place where company management and public relations representatives may spend time posting jobs or promoting news about their brand. This can help job seekers to know more about a place before they apply for an open position. It can also help anyone interested in a company for any other reason to learn more about what that company does. Since many businesses are active on the network, it is easy for employees to find and link to their current and former employers when they create an account. By

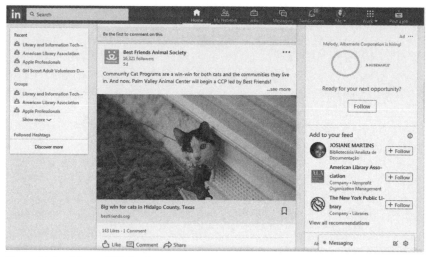

Figure 8.1.   View of LinkedIn.

doing so, LinkedIn can suggest possible contacts to new LinkedIn users—usually current and former employees of the same companies. Also, anyone looking at someone's profile can click on current and former employers to see more about those companies, as well as current employees who also have LinkedIn accounts. Overall, using LinkedIn is a great way to learn more about companies and the professional lives of people, as well as a place to share your own professional accomplishments.

WHY DO PEOPLE USE LINKEDIN?

People at all stages of their career, including retired people or those not looking for a job, may find LinkedIn valuable as a professional network. People have many possible professional contacts, including current coworkers, former coworkers, project partners from other organizations, and those in the same field who they meet at conferences and trainings. Old classmates and even teachers are also in a person's professional network. Sometimes people do not want to connect with these people on personal social media accounts, like Facebook, because they do not want to share details about their family and personal life with such a broad audience. However, it can be helpful to stay connected to people who fit into these categories as they move through their careers and lives. LinkedIn provides a way to do that.

Being connected to professional contacts does not mean that you cannot also link to family and friends on LinkedIn. You can. In fact, it is often a way to know professional details about a family member that you might not otherwise know. Family members sometimes do not share professional accomplishments in the same way that colleagues or classmates might. Consider, for example, whether you know what professional certifications a cousin has, or whether a niece or nephew is looking for a new job. These same family members might post photos and personal news on Instagram or Facebook, but LinkedIn is a place to keep up with them professionally.

Those starting out in their career and those looking for a job are a significant part of LinkedIn's audience. More than 500 million professionals were passively or actively job seeking on the network in late 2018.[3] The platform offers numerous tools for connecting companies with possible employees. Users can openly or privately set their account settings to allow recruiters to know that they are looking for a job. If their account profile is up to date, recruiters can browse their education and experience easily to see if a candidate is a good match for their position. Even those who are not actively looking may enjoy seeing what jobs are available as a future-planning exercise. For more proactive job seekers, LinkedIn facilitates applying for open positions right on the site. Employers can post jobs on LinkedIn, and users can search and apply within the platform interface. In addition, users can limit their job search or alerts to only certain companies, allowing them to selectively see jobs that interest them or just to know when their dream job opens.

Those who are in a job and not looking to change still get value from LinkedIn by using it to keep up with professional contacts. Some people keep professional contacts in their phone or e-mail contact list, where they are mixed with personal contacts. This isn't ideal for some people. Others may keep their professional contacts in their work accounts. However, what happens when they switch jobs? Keeping up with people that you meet in classes, at conferences, or on projects can be helpful, even as you move around throughout a career. If you move to a new city, you can check LinkedIn to see what former classmates or contacts have also ended up there. You can also check to see if you have second-degree contacts (people who know someone that you know) at your new company. Building a strong network helps with transitions and also helps others know where you are and what you are doing.

Tracking professional highlights, education, connections, recommendations, and skills can be a helpful feature of LinkedIn, and it can help a future employer know what experience a person has. While an individual résumé or curriculum vitae may have selected experience and skills listed to highlight certain involvement, LinkedIn users can update their profile with all of their accomplishments. It can be difficult to remember employment dates, class details, and job titles years after a position was held, so putting all this information on LinkedIn may help people recall that information later. LinkedIn users can also receive endorsements and recommendations from others on the platform. Endorsements happen when people in a user's professional network publicly agree that the person has a skill. So, if someone is amazing at Adobe Photoshop, others who have witnessed their work using Photoshop can endorse that skill. The number of people who have endorsed a skill appears next to the skill in the user's LinkedIn profile, so everyone can see when someone has multiple endorsements for it. Similarly, LinkedIn connections who want to write a full recommendation of a person and their work can do so on LinkedIn. Recommendations also appear in a user's profile.

While building and maintaining a user profile is part of the basic LinkedIn experience, many users get more from the platform. Though not everyone uses them, LinkedIn has features that allow their users to post news and write articles on the site. Influencers—those who have a large following on LinkedIn—post often to establish themselves as news leaders in their area of interest. Other features on LinkedIn focus on premium (paid) account users who may be in sales, human resources, or marketing. If you are in these lines of work, you can use LinkedIn differently and can take advantage of the many upgraded features that allow you to identify leads and connections.

Even retirees may enjoy LinkedIn. Some retired people might want to follow former coworkers and employers to see news and changes. Though their career may not be active, retirees may enjoy having their awards, career highlights, and professional endorsements available online. Alumni networks are active on the platform, as are many interest groups, and retired people may enjoy that interaction. Many retirees may also be involved with organizations that value their previous professional experience. For example, users serving on a nonprofit board or doing occasional public speaking may want people to know what they did in previous roles. Finally, LinkedIn is sometimes the best way to keep up with former colleagues and professional connections as they move around from different employers through their career. If someone does not want to connect to them on more personal networks like Facebook, LinkedIn is a good choice for these professional connections.

LINKEDIN TERMINOLOGY

Company Page—This is a LinkedIn page for a company or employer. It is different in several ways from a profile page, which individual users can have. A company page includes a company summary and other pertinent details about the organization. It also contains a link to current employees who have LinkedIn pages. In the case of schools, it also links to alumni who have included the school on their profile. LinkedIn users can follow a company to keep up with news and job announcements.

Connection—This is the LinkedIn term for people who are in your network. Connections are listed by degree, with people you have connected to directly being first-degree connections. People who are in the same group as a user are also in their network.

Degree of Connection—Connections in your LinkedIn network can be first-, second-, or third-degree connections. These designations will appear next to a user's name when someone searches LinkedIn or looks at a list of employees at a company. First-degree connections are people who someone has directly linked to on the site. Second-degree connections share a first-degree connection with the user. Third-degree connections are connected to a second-degree connection of the user. LinkedIn users can connect with second-degree connections easily but may not be able to connect to third-degree connections or see their full names depending on privacy settings.

Endorsement—A skill or quality that someone in your network says that someone has. Multiple people can endorse a user for the same skill, which reinforces that user's experience or expertise in that area. Endorsements appear in a user's profile page and are separated into categories, including Industry Knowledge, Tools and Technologies, and Interpersonal Skills. Users can add their own skills to their profile but cannot endorse themselves.

Group—Groups are collections of people interested in a shared topic and organized on LinkedIn to discuss or connect around that topic.

Influencer—Influencers are people with a large following, such as Oprah Winfrey or Arianna Huffington. The *influencer* designation is offered by LinkedIn to specific users and cannot be purchased or applied for through other means.

Introduction—Users who know two unconnected individuals on the platform can introduce them to one another, allowing them to become connections when they were previously out of network to one another.

Message—When someone is a third connection or out of network, premium users (those who have paid accounts) can directly message that user to ask for a connection.

Network / Out of Network—A user's network on LinkedIn includes their direct connections (first degree), people their connections know (second degree), and people those people know (third degree). Members of shared groups are also in a user's network.

Post—Similar to other platforms, LinkedIn users can add a comment or share news by adding a post from the home screen in their account. Some LinkedIn users never post and only take advantage of job-search or profile-sharing features. Others may post often to establish themselves as a contributor to professional dialogue in their field.

Premium—LinkedIn Premium is the upgraded version of the social media platform. It offers many features that are not available to basic (free) accounts, including being able to see who views your profile, connecting with users who are out of network, and increased job-seeking options.

Recommendation—While users can endorse one another's skills, recommendations are in-depth reviews of an individual's work or experience. Recommendations appear in paragraph form and include the name and image of the person who wrote the recommendation. They appear in the LinkedIn user profile of the subject of the recommendation.

Skills—Users can list skills that they possess in their user profile. If their connections agree that the user possesses that skill, they can endorse the skill. This indicates to others on LinkedIn that the user really is knowledgeable in that area of expertise. Multiple users can endorse the same skill for the same user, and the number of endorsements appears next to the skill in the user's profile.

THE BASICS OF USING LINKEDIN

Creating a LinkedIn page is straightforward. New users will need to provide an e-mail or phone number, as well as their real name. The platform's user agreement requires that people use their real names on the network. Users must also be at least 16 years old. LinkedIn will guide new users through a series of questions, with some details being required and others not. Students will have their own menu that helps them choose their school and field. Nonstudents can list their current employer and position, as well as their industry and other details. Once users create an account, they will want to add additional professional experience and education to their user profile. Unlike many other networks,

LinkedIn user profiles are not overly creative. Instead, they focus on clear details about a person's professional work by entering details into structured areas within their profiles.

The LinkedIn account screen consists of a Home feed, My Network, Jobs, Messaging, and Notifications, which all show up at the top of the screen (see figure 8.2). The mobile app has comparable features and options along the bottom of the screen (see figure 8.3). The Home feed is where users will see news from their connections, groups that they join, schools they attended, influencers they follow, and companies they follow. On the browser version, people will also see suggestions for other companies or people they may wish to follow. My Network shows a user's connections, current invitations to connect, and suggestions for new connections. It also recommends groups, companies, and hashtags that a user may be interested in, based on their other connections.

The Jobs area of LinkedIn has many features, primarily for job hunters and those posting jobs. However, even people who are not actively job hunting can browse similar positions or check LinkedIn Salary to see what other careers and positions are earning in a specific geographic area. LinkedIn lets job hunters

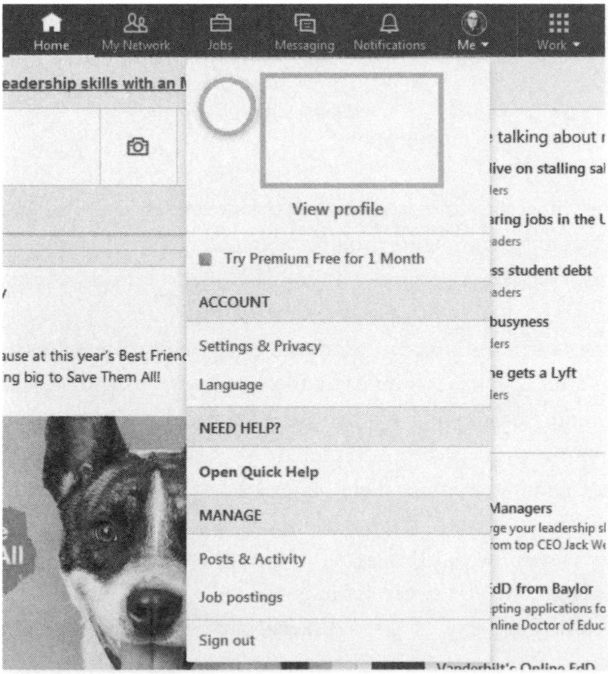

Figure 8.2.   Viewing LinkedIn options on a computer.

Figure 8.3. Viewing LinkedIn options on the mobile app.

indicate their interest in finding a new job. Once turned on, this feature will take skills and experience from your profile and match it with open positions that are not at that user's current company. It will also suggest hiring companies where the LinkedIn user already has connections.

Messaging is where LinkedIn users can have private message conversations with one another. This is where users may reach out to a professional contact when they might be moving to their area or company or when they have a question about a project they completed. Messaging is also where LinkedIn and advertisers may send you offers. These messages will be clearly marked as "LinkedIn Offer" at the top of the message. When users have invited a new person to connect with them, Messaging is also where a confirmation will appear when the user accepts the connection.

The Notifications area of LinkedIn will alert users to work anniversaries, new jobs, and other news from their connections. It will also be where users see responses to their own news or posts and where viewing activity shows up (how many people have viewed a user's profile). LinkedIn users have control over what notifications they want to receive and can make adjustments at the individual or account level. For individual notifications that appear in their account, they can click on the three-dot menu next to the notification to delete the message, unfollow news from or about that person, or turn off similar notifications. By clicking on View Settings in the sidebar, users can adjust their overall notification settings to meet their needs. Recommendations for people to follow, connection anniversaries, responses to job updates, and many more items can be turned on or off in the Notifications settings (see figure 8.4).

LinkedIn offers a search bar where users can look for keywords, people, or company names. Search results will be organized into categories, including

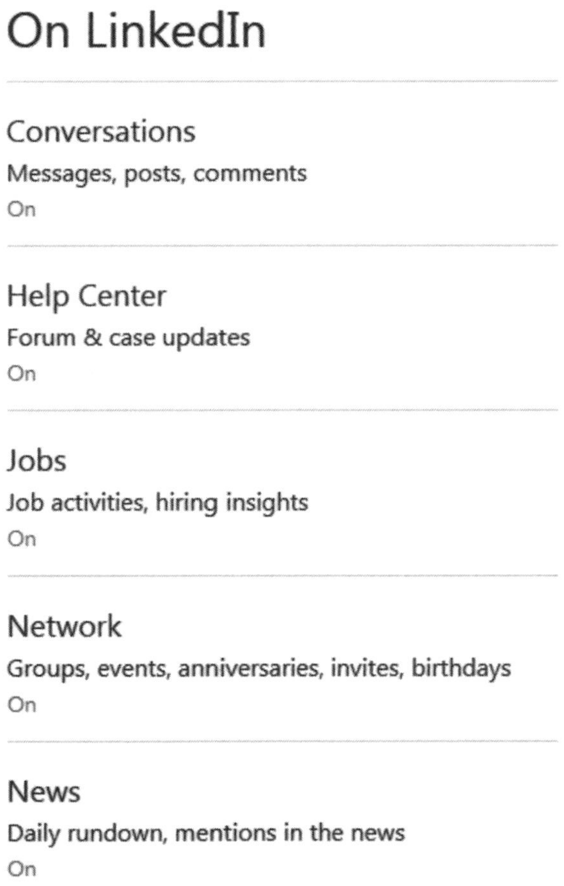

On LinkedIn

Conversations
Messages, posts, comments
On

Help Center
Forum & case updates
On

Jobs
Job activities, hiring insights
On

Network
Groups, events, anniversaries, invites, birthdays
On

News
Daily rundown, mentions in the news
On

Figure 8.4. LinkedIn notification settings.

open jobs, people, and companies. It will also give similar terms to search. If users want to find a nonspecific person (such as someone in their network who works in a field or has that keyword in their profile), they can limit the list by how close of a connection someone should be. For example, if you need a realtor you may search for realtors and then include second-degree connections; this will give you all the realtors that your direct (first-degree) connections know. Limiting by the location as well is an easy way to narrow down to a list of professionals for your project or interest.

Clicking on the Me menu will give users a drop-down menu of settings and account help (see figure 8.5). This is where users can update their profile and change settings for search and privacy, among other things. Users can update their account information (such as e-mail and phone number), as well as site preferences and communications. As previously mentioned, some of these notifications are also available from other areas of the site. By clicking on View Profile under Me, users can see how their profile looks to other people. The More feature lets users share their profile or save it as a PDF.

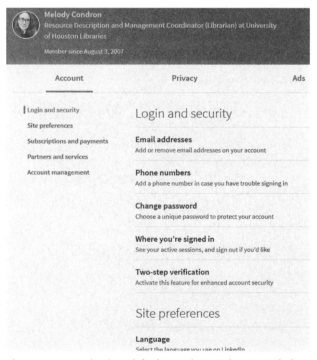

Figure 8.5.   Reviewing LinkedIn settings and account help.

PRIVACY AND SAFETY

LinkedIn is not a place for people who want to be overly private. Basic profile information is publicly available for everyone to view. The idea, of course, is that the information posted on the site is mainly professional, and much of that may be publicly available already. Still, anything that people post in their LinkedIn profile is easily found by companies and individuals, and it is probably also collected for use on other sites through data scraping.[4] Users should remain professional and include only information that they are willing to share with anyone on the web on their LinkedIn profile.

LinkedIn requires the use of true names. This rule, which is part of the user agreement and terms of use for the site, exists to ensure the professional usefulness of the site and encourages connections between business associates who use their real names.[5] This does mean that users are generally who they say they are; although someone could create a false account, there are not many benefits to doing so because of the nature of the site. The downside to the use of true names is that users must divulge who they are and cannot create anonymous accounts, as they can with other social media networks. If someone wants to participate on LinkedIn, they should be committed to using their real name in order to follow the site's user agreement.

Despite the relatively public nature of user profiles, many of LinkedIn's job-searching options are mainly private. For obvious reasons, many of the features that allow users to privately look for jobs without letting their current employer know are private. LinkedIn ensures users that applying for a job through the site or the LinkedIn Job Search Mobile App is private. Also, others in your network will not know you are looking for a new position unless you post that information to them.[6] Users can also turn on the option in their profile that allows recruiters to know that they are open to opportunities (see figure 8.6). However, this feature is not as secure. LinkedIn offers the warning: "We take steps not to show your current company that you're open, but can't guarantee complete privacy." If this option makes users nervous, they might instead choose to use the option that shares job interest only with approved employers. That means that the LinkedIn user can create a list of target companies that they are open to for recruitment.

Some Safety Tips for LinkedIn

- While it can be exciting and encouraging to connect to as many people as possible on a professional network, many users do not accept every connection invite they receive. Marketers and distant contacts may try to connect to you even though they do not actually know you professionally, and it is okay to decline or ignore these requests.

- Both for your own privacy and the privacy of others, review your personal contacts before you agree to LinkedIn's Add Personal Contacts feature. Using the function will invite all your e-mail contacts to link to you or to join the network if they are not already on it. It may not make sense to add all contacts to a professional network. For example, your 13-year-old nephew and your elderly neighbor may not appreciate the e-mails, though they may be in your contact list.

- Account settings under Privacy allow users to control who can see the e-mail account linked to their LinkedIn profile. Users who have created an account using a personal e-mail address should consider limiting access or changing to a professional e-mail address for their account.

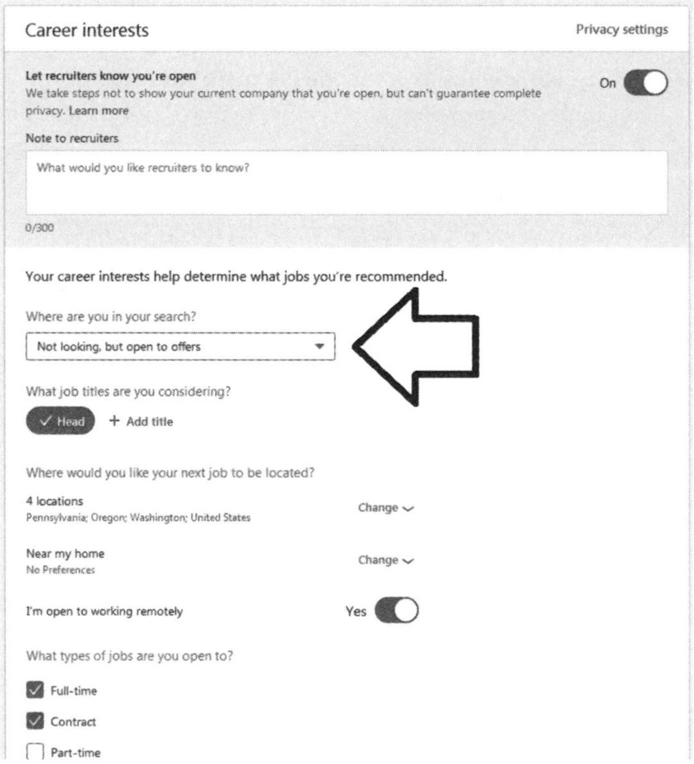

Figure 8.6. Making yourself available to recruiting opportunities on LinkedIn.

SPECIAL FEATURES AND HELP

Using LinkedIn as an online résumé can be helpful to many users. LinkedIn is a great place to track all professional experience and skills and, as such, is a great place to start if someone needs to build a résumé or curriculum vitae and keep track of the courses, certificates, dates, and other details of past professional experience in some other manner. Users who have kept their account up to date can download their profile information as a PDF and easily copy it into another document as a starting point for a résumé.

Advertising control is an interesting feature of LinkedIn and offers many options to those who are interested. Users on the site have the option to turn on or off several features that will change what advertisements and job leads they will see. By clicking on their profile image > Settings and Privacy > Ads, LinkedIn users can turn the following advertising-controlling options on or off: interest categories, use of websites outside of LinkedIn, a user's LinkedIn connections, companies a user follows, user education, and more. If someone is bothered by the idea of receiving advertising based on their demographics or web use, then they can choose to turn it off.

TUMBLR

Tumblr is a social blogging platform where users create what is usually called microblogs: short, frequent posts that can be followed by other users. Lifewire describes it as similar to Twitter but with "fewer limitations and more features."[1] Tumblr offers themed website backgrounds and many other tools to help people make unique and visually interesting *tumblogs* (Tumblr + blogs). Posts can be images, links, audio, video, or text. Posts to the same Tumblr feed are often (but not always) similar in subject matter, unlike many personal social media accounts where someone may post about more random topics. People can also create multiple tumblogs that can be managed through one account. Once someone joins Tumblr, they can follow multiple tumblogs in a feed, similarly to other social media. A tumblog can also be viewed as its own website, with its own web address. That means that public tumblogs can be viewed by anyone, with or without a Tumblr account.

WHY DO PEOPLE USE TUMBLR?

As of spring 2019, Tumblr reports having more than 459 million blogs on its platform (see figure 9.1).[2] Tumblr is built for people who want to keep a blog or online journal but do not want to write long posts. Because tumblogs offer built-in features for highlighting different kinds of posts (for example, quotes, audio, links), it may be easier for new bloggers than setting up on another platform. Almost anything that someone might want to share with a specific or public audience could fit on Tumblr. Some examples of common microblogging page content include food and cooking images and restaurant reviews; travel photos and updates from a trip; hobby blogging about knitting, Lego building; DIY (do it yourself); and tips and commentary on parenting, life, music, and more.

People use Tumblr much in the same way that they would use any blog: to post regular content to friends, family, or the public on a variety of topics. The difference with Tumblr is that posts are generally short or media based. Hypothetically that means that people can review and stay up with a tumblog easily, since there are no long stories or content. Like Twitter, people are attracted to the short posts and ease of sharing things they find that they like. If you have a Tumblr account, you can follow many microbloggers at once and see all of their posts together in one place. However, many people would not notice much difference between a Tumblr blog and a website if they are viewed by going directly to the tumblog address. This is why many tumblogs serve a specific purpose for their creator that is meant to reach far beyond the Tumblr platform. For example, an art portfolio could be accessible to anyone on the web, while also encouraging traffic by making it easy to share the art on Tumblr.

Though many people think about blogs as being personal sharing spaces, Tumblr isn't full of personal writing. Some users do not post things that they

Tumblr is so easy to use that it's hard to explain.

We made it really, really simple for people to make a blog and put whatever they want on it. Stories, photos, GIFs, TV shows, links, quips, dumb jokes, smart jokes, Spotify tracks, mp3s, videos, fashion, art, deep stuff. Tumblr is 459 million different blogs, filled with literally whatever.

Figure 9.1. Tumblr hosts more than 450 million blogs.

have created themselves, preferring instead to share things they like and found elsewhere. Again, the built-in functionality of adding a quote, a link, and reblogging others' posts makes Tumblr a great site for this sort of sharing. Like many other platforms, Tumblr has many tumblogs that feature memes and GIFs that users want to share with their friends. These can be things that are found anywhere, or on Tumblr—or even a mix of both. That gives Tumblr creators a lot of freedom to create and collect things that they like into one digital space.

Since many tumblogs share a lot of images, Tumblr can be used similarly to Instagram. Many people use it the same way as Instagram but prefer the platform because they can post nonimage posts, like quotes and links, when they need to. Tumblr bloggers can create a stylized page that is more unique and individualized. Photographers and other artists use the site as a portfolio space, where they can share their work in a way that looks professionally curated. Also like Instagram, Tumblr users may create a microblog that just appeals to their small, specific audience: something that is really just a way of interacting with friends and sharing inside jokes. Tumblogs can be set to private for users who want to share in this way. This sort of Tumblr use makes it a lot more like other social networks.

For others, Tumblr is a place to create weird and specific collections of media. It is easy to have multiple tumblogs going at once, so people can create many things that they add to as they see content that applies. Tumblr users may browse lots of things on Tumblr and pick and choose the things they want for their blogs. For example, they may follow lots of superhero-themed tumblogs and choose individual posts about a specific character or actress that they can reblog (add to their blog) on a fan page. They may also add their own artwork about the character, movie quotes, links to movie clips, or soundtrack clips. This has led to a lot of nostalgia or fan blogs devoted to one person, band, or topic. In that way, it is more like Pinterest—a scrapbook of content that is created by many different people, collected and curated in one place. Reblogging on Tumblr is so easy that popular items are passed around the site easily.

Because it is user friendly and free, Tumblr can also be used instead of making a traditionally hosted website. There are many themes provided by the site. Also, the mobile app makes it easy to add content to a Tumblr site when you don't have access to a computer. Users can even change their Tumblr URL to a custom domain in their account settings, so that they can choose a web address that isn't a Tumblr subdomain. This makes it possible for businesses and professionals who use the site to keep a website name consistent, even if they want to leave Tumblr at some point in the future.

TUMBLR TERMINOLOGY

Add to Queue—This is an option when posting on Tumblr. It allows you to add the post in the line of other posts you have already created and post them at intervals. This helps a blog to stay active and have regularly posted content, rather than be active a lot in short intervals and quiet for long periods in between. You can see posts in your queue by clicking on the account icon, then the three-dot menu and clicking Queue.

Avatar—An avatar is the image you use to represent yourself on your blog. It is the small image that commonly appears next to your posts and at the top of your page. It can be turned off or changed by going to account (the little person icon)> Edit Appearance > Edit Theme. Clicking on the pencil next to the avatar will let you change the image, or you can turn it off in the same menu.

Blog—Short for a web log, blogs are websites or other online posting locations where someone regularly posts updates in an informal style. Unlike articles or news stories, blogs are usually more conversational.

Dashboard—The dashboard is one of two places where you will spend a lot of time on Tumblr (the other is your blog page). It is where you will see posts from all the blogs that you follow, suggestions for new things to check out, and navigation for all the Tumblr pages you manage.

Feed—Your feed is the content from other tumblogs that appears in your dashboard. Users can scroll through the content to see all the posts from Tumblrs they follow, as well as some that are suggested by Tumblr.

Follow—As with other social media platforms, you can choose to follow other users so you see their posts. To follow people on Tumblr, simply click on the blue Follow button while looking at another user's account, or while browsing in search.

GPOY—GPOY is an acronym for Gratuitous Picture of Yourself, something that is common on Tumblr. Entire tumblogs may be full of GPOY posts, or someone may just post one occasionally.

Microblog / Microblogging—A microblog is a place where users post short, frequent content.

Notes—Notes include likes, comments, and reblogs from other users. The total number of notes is listed under a Tumblr post, and you can click on the total to see all notes.

Permalink—This is a unique URL web address link that goes to a specific blog post on Tumblr. It can be shared so that people can go directly to a specific post.

Photo Reply—This is a feature you can turn on to allow users to reply to your posts with images instead of words.

Post—A post is the content you add to your microblog on Tumblr, including an audio clip, an image, or text.

Reblog—Using the reblog icon at the bottom of a post will post it to your feed.

Schedule Blog—For those who want to post at certain times or intervals, Tumblr allows bloggers to schedule their posts as they are created. Users can click Post and then Schedule from the menu to do this. This means that users should be aware that not all posts are created right when they are posted. To schedule a new post, click on the arrow next to Post and choose Schedule. You can type in the time you would like the post to be published and then click on Schedule.

#Tag—Short for hashtag, tags are keywords starting with a # that are added to Tumblr posts. You can search Tumblr or individual blogs by tag. Tags are linked on Tumblr, so users can click on them to see additional posts with the same tag.

Themes—Themes are customizable background and styles for a Tumblr blog. They control how a tumblog will look when viewed at its blog address. However, the theme does not appear when posts are shown in a dashboard feed. Blog themes can be changed in account settings under Edit Appearance.

Tumblog | Tumblr—These are names for a blog on Tumblr.

THE BASICS OF USING TUMBLR

You will only need an e-mail address to set up an account on Tumblr. Users will also create a Tumblr name and password. The name will be used as the name of the user's first (and primary) tumblog, and it will appear in the Tumblr web address for their blog. For example, the name *animals* would have a tumblog at https://animals.tumblr.com/. Once you have confirmed your e-mail address, you can start browsing and following other Tumblrs, or you can create your own.

There are some important differences between your primary (first) blog and secondary blogs. You can create up to 10 secondary blogs a day on Tumblr, and each can have different settings and themes. Secondary blogs can also have multiple users, so you could share a blog with other people. Secondary blogs can also be password protected so that only certain people who have been invited can view the content. Your primary blog cannot have multiple users or be password protected, so plan ahead for how you want to use your primary blog. For example, don't choose a blog name that you want to be private for your primary blog, since it cannot be password protected. To see more about the differences between primary and secondary blogs, visit the Tumblr Help Center by clicking on Account (the icon looks like a little person), then Help.

After creating an account, users can start creating and posting to their tumblog. Most of the account options appear in the Account menu, which is split into two sections: Account and Tumblrs (see figure 9.2). The account options show likes, others you are following, overall account settings, and help. All of your blogs will appear under Tumblrs. You can create a new Tumblr page by clicking +New, or you can click on any of the options below primary Tumblr name. Clicking on Edit Appearance will show options for changing the blog theme and other settings specific to that tumblog. The Edit Theme button will take you to a screen with multiple layout options for your blog. You can change your avatar, header image, layout, color scheme, and much more in the Edit Theme layout screen.

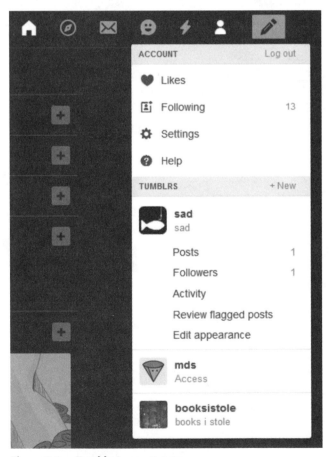

Figure 9.2.   Tumblr Account menu.

Once you have designed your Tumblr the way that you want it, you are ready to add posts. You can create your own posts, or browse around and reblog things that you find on other people's blogs. If you want to create your own content to post, you can choose from GIF, link, audio, video, quote, photo, or text. In the mobile app, you can add a post by clicking on the pencil icon at the bottom of the screen (see figure 9.3). On a computer, the same posting options appear at the top of the Home Feed screen, and when clicking on the pencil icon at the top right of the screen (see figure 9.4). Each of the different kinds of posts has different format options specific to the theme you have chosen for the blog. If you change the theme later, posts of a certain type will change in the same way for consistency. Be aware: posting text allows you to add additional media with the text, while posting other media directly does not always allow you to also add text in the same way as the text option.

Pay attention to the options available in the Post screen for extra features. If you have more than one Tumblr blog, make sure you are posting to the one that you want by selecting it in the drop-down menu at the top of the screen.

Figure 9.3. Choose the pencil icon on the mobile Tumblr app to post.

Figure 9.4. Choose the pencil icon on the upper right of the computer screen to post.

On the upper right of the screen when posting via computer, you will find some interesting technical options including changing the post's URL and post date. These options will allow you to change the post date to a different date, such as last week or last year. Changing the URL may be helpful if you want a specific permalink for the specific blog you are posting. These options appear along the bottom of the screen when using the iOS or Android Mobile app (see figure 9.5). On the lower right of the Post window on the computer, you can control whether to post now, add to your queue (these will be posted at intervals), save as a draft, or schedule for a specific date and time (see figure 9.6). You can also post privately (more on that in the "Privacy and Safety" section of this chapter). The same options appear on the mobile app when you click on the gear icon. Finally, you can add hashtags (usually just called #tags on Tumblr) to help others find your post by keyword. Once you post, it will appear on your blog, which you can see in Tumblr by clicking on your avatar (user image), or by going to your Tumblr URL (yourusername.tumblr.com).

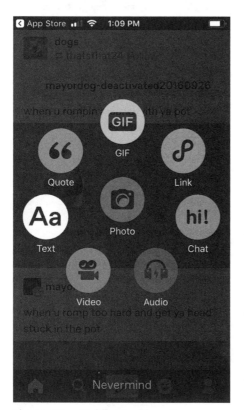

Figure 9.5. Mobile Tumblr options.

Users who are not ready to post yet may just want to browse around Tumblr to see what others are doing. You can use the Search Tumblr field at the top of the Home screen on a computer, or click on the magnifying glass icon in the app to search. When viewing on a computer, you can click on the compass icon to explore Tumblr by what is trending, staff picks, and other popular media. Tumblr may also recommend blogs it thinks you will enjoy, which will appear under a Recommended Blogs menu option. Clicking on the avatar next to any post will show you that person's Tumblr feed, and you can choose to follow them. You can click on the + or Follow button to start following a blog you like. If you find a specific post you like, you can reblog it to your own Tumblr by clicking on the two ar-

Figure 9.6. Computer Tumblr options.

rows circling icon that appears below every post. You can also like things by clicking on the heart, or comment on a post by clicking on the word *bubble*. The paper airplane icon will let you share the post on other social media or report the post for inappropriate content.

You can return home to your dashboard by clicking on the house icon in the app or on the computer. Your dashboard feed will show you posts from feeds that you follow and is organized by Tumblr to show you things that you like the most. This is based on previous history. If you would prefer a chronological feed, you can change the setting in account settings. Like Twitter and many other social media platforms, the dashboard feed has continuous scroll, so you can keep scrolling down and more posts will appear. With millions of tumblogs available, users should have no trouble finding something of interest to follow.

PRIVACY AND SAFETY

Tumblogs have a number of privacy and safety options. Secondary tumblogs can be set to private when they are created (or later through settings). Private blogs require a password to view. The password is set by the creator, and it can be changed periodically to maintain security. It is important to remember that anyone with the blog address and password can access the blog. That means that anyone who gets access could choose to share it with other people who were not invited directly from the blog creator. Unfortunately, primary Tumblr names cannot be set to private. However, there is nothing requiring Tumblr users to post to that blog. Users could easily set up their primary name and keep it empty, while posting to a secondary private blog. Alternatively, you can also make individual posts (including those on the primary Tumblr) private. However, this does not mean the same thing as a private blog. Private posts can only be seen by other administrators on a group blog or by the creator. This may be helpful to some users who want to keep things for their own special projects or who participate in group projects. However, it does not create private posts that can be shared with specific users.

It may also be helpful to some users to know that the rules for adult content on Tumblr have recently changed. Until late 2018, Tumblr was a popular site for pornographic content. That is no longer the case. Tumblr gave existing accounts warning that adult content would be removed in fall 2018, and the site is now running an algorithm to identify and remove it. Some have been happy with the change. However, artists and others have complained that the new rules limit free speech. Other have complained that the algorithms that are meant to identify adult content have incorrectly flagged many unrelated images.[3] No matter your feelings on the subject, Tumblr encourages people to report anything that they think should not be on the site. Tumblr users can report a post by clicking on the paper airplane icon below the post and clicking on Report.

Some Tumblr Privacy and Safety Tips

- By going to Account and clicking on Privacy, you can see a few of the options available. Most notably, you can toggle off the button that lets other people see when you are active on the platform. You can also choose whether you will allow Tumblr to track your searching.
- If there are specific topics or names that you do not want to see on Tumblr, you can use the tag filter. You can do this no matter what the reason—whether you are trying to avoid television show spoilers or avoiding mentions of famous people who annoy you. The tag filter option is available from the main Account screen when you click on the account (little person) icon. Users can click on the little pencil to add tags they do not want to see.
- In the Edit Appearance menu for a specific tumblog, you can change who can reply to your posts. The default setting is for anyone to be able to reply to your posts, but it can be changed. You can decide if only Tumblrs you follow can reply or if Tumblrs you follow plus those who have followed you for a week can reply.

FUN FEATURES

Tumblr Labs is a feature that users can turn on and off if they want to be early adopters/experiencers of new Tumblr features. Tumblr describes labs as "a col-

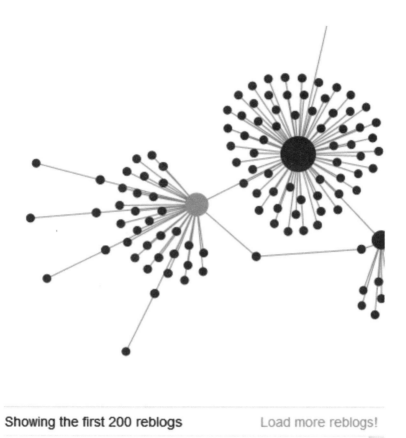

Showing the first 200 reblogs   Load more reblogs!

Figure 9.7.   The Tumblr Lab reblog graph.

lection of experiments we're working on that might turn out to be useful, fun, both, or neither."[4] To see some of the latest experiments and opt in, click on the account/user icon (it looks like a little person), then Settings, then Labs. Some early 2019 labs include reblog graphs that track how a blog travels through Tumblr (see figure 9.7), as well as an Emojify option that replaces some blog post words with emojis.[5]

"*Lesser-Known Features*" is a section of the Tumblr Help Center that tells you about hotkeys, tools, and tricks that might not be immediately obvious. iOS-specific app tricks like the "touch and hold a photo" option or Android-specific features like "bump phones to share blogs" are described on this Help Center page. Tumblr adds new features to the page as needed, so it does not hurt to review them even if you have been using Tumblr for a while. To navigate to the page, go to the account icon, then Help, and search for "Lesser-Known Features."

PINTEREST

Pinterest is a social media platform where users, sometimes called *pinners*, can create *pinboards* where they collect images and short videos from all over the internet or from other boards on Pinterest. They can share these boards publicly or keep them private. Pinterest users can follow one another's boards and can search for images that they want to pin to their own boards. Each user can have multiple boards, which are often themed by subject, such as animals, recipes, or funny memes. The site is used heavily by crafters, hobbyists, artists, decorators, and others who want to keep and collect images that they like on a specific topic. Since the images are not stored on Pinterest but are pulled in from their locations all over the web, users can pin items to their boards that they do not own.[1] Users can also pin their own photos or a website to a board, although this is less common. Some users may use Pinterest as a bookmarking tool to keep images they want to refer to later. Common internet browsers have a plugin that allows pinners to add a Pinterest button at the top of the page so that they can pin images to their boards when they are browsing the web. Images pinned from the web retain links that will take people back to the image's original website, so it is possible to promote a person or site by pinning their images.[2]

Pinterest is unlike many other social media sites because it shares and collects existing images from all over the web rather than focusing on newly created content by the person using the site (see figure 10.1). Pinterest users pin things of interest (hence the name)—and collecting and sharing those things is the main activity, not sharing their own thoughts, opinions, or personally created images (although some people do use Pinterest that way, too—it is just not as common as on other sites). This different focus means that pinners end up using the

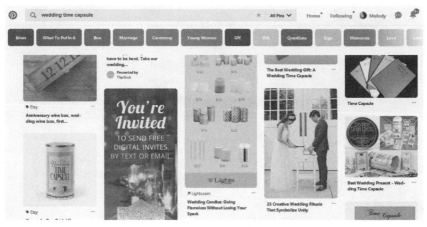

Figure 10.1. View of Pinterest.

network in a very different way than they use other social media. For example, many users create boards for projects or personal uses rather than using Pinterest to keep up with friends and family. Also, although the site does allow users to pin GIFs and short videos, the images do not move while viewing them on a pinboard—someone must click through to the main image to see video. As a result, still images are much more common on the site than moving images.

WHY DO PEOPLE USE PINTEREST?

Pinterest is all about collecting and sharing images from all over the web. Unlike Flickr and Instagram, Pinterest images are often not created by the person using the social media platform. As a result, Pinterest is a place where people collect and share images they like. Pinboards may be as simple as a collection of images someone likes, such as photographs they find pretty or cute pictures of dogs (or a mix of these things together). Casual Pinterest users may decide to just have one board where they collect all images, as they might with other social media like Twitter or Facebook. However, since pinners can have multiple boards in their accounts (the limit is 500 boards, or 200,000 images), most pinners create multiple boards with themes.

The most basic way pinners use Pinterest is to collect images they like, as they find them. Pinning them to public or private boards shares the images with other users, who may re-pin the items to their own boards if they also like them.

Sharing can be with friends and family who can find and follow another person's board. If the board is public, then anyone from across the site can see and re-pin images that a user has collected and pinned to their boards. Once people start posting, Pinterest will also suggest boards to follow and images similar to those already collected. Though Pinterest is image based, not all images are photos and art. Recipes and memes are also quite common on Pinterest. For example, mommy blogs and parenting magazines have highlighted Pinterest as a place to do meal planning, where parents can browse and share recipes to try out later. Sharing funny images or even news headlines is also not uncommon on the site; creating fan pages for a television show, actor, or band is also popular. For example, searching for *Stranger Things* on Pinterest will show a variety of boards devoted to fan art and photos of the actors from the Netflix show.

Many Pinterest boards are devoted to a specific project that someone is planning, such as a new home or a wedding. Pinterest pages for weddings are so common that bridal magazines all have Pinterest boards.[3] In these cases, the board often serves as a place to collect and store ideas. Like the look of a certain dress or the decorations in a style magazine feature? Pin them to a board. Building a new home or remodeling a kitchen? Pin images from architecture blogs or from other architecture buffs who have pages on Pinterest. Because multiple people can share a board, this is a great way to brainstorm about an upcoming project so that people have ideas to discuss.

Pinterest can also be a way to promote an artist or project. To do that, the artist must already have images posted elsewhere on the web. Using the browser plugin button, Pinterest users who like the art or image can pin and share it, usually with a link attached that will draw traffic back to the original site. Galleries and others with a public project that have photo or image updates may want to go to their website where images are posted and then pin them to Pinterest boards for greater exposure.

Many businesses, organizations, and groups have also found fun ways to use Pinterest. Greyhound (the American bus service) offers Pinterest pages of the best games and books for long-distance travel. Churches and family groups may collect images of fun activities and crafts to do with kids. Some businesses may also be using Pinterest to sell products through paid advertising on the site. This sort of image, which will look similar to a regular image post, will say "Promoted" at the bottom. Pinners can still pin a promoted image to their board—in fact, that is what the advertiser is hoping will happen. If someone loves the item or image, they may click through and purchase it. Keep in mind that commercial users of Pinterest must register using a business account.[4]

PINTEREST TERMINOLOGY

Board / Pinboard—Pinterest users have one or more collections of images and short video called boards or pinboards where they can post and share images and short videos. Many compare these collections to a digital bulletin board where people can pin their items for others to see.

Follow—You can follow other users or a specific pinboard by clicking on a user's name. To see all of their future posts, click on the Follow button.

Hashtag—A hashtag is a keyword or phrase without spaces that starts with a hash/number [#] symbol in front of it. Searching for a hashtag helps people find images on social media and across the internet. Hashtags in the captions and comments of Pinterest images are linked automatically. Clicking on a linked hashtag in a comment or searching for it in the search box will show all Pinterest posts that use the same hashtag.

Home—The Home screen is where you can see images from all the people and boards you follow, as well as images that Pinterest chooses for you to see based on what you post on your boards. You can click the Pinterest P in the upper left (in a computer browser) or in the lower left (on mobile) to go to your Home screen.

Mention—Pinterest users can mention another user's Twitter handle in a Pinterest image comment by using that user's Twitter username (@username). However, the name is not automatically linked on Pinterest.

Pin / Re-pin—When you add an image to one of your boards, you *pin* it. You can also *re-pin* an item by pinning an image someone else added to their collection to your own pinboard.

Pinner—This is a slang term for a person on Pinterest.

Secret Boards—These are Pinterest boards that have been set as private. They will appear in their own section when you click on your boards. Only you and people you invite can see Secret Boards on Pinterest.

Send—You can click on any Pinterest image to see it larger. There, you can click the Send button to share the image with specific Pinterest users or on other platforms, including WhatsApp, Facebook, or Twitter. You can also use Send to copy a direct link to the image on Pinterest or to e-mail a link.

THE BASICS OF USING PINTEREST

Creating an account on Pinterest.com is straightforward and free. Users will need an e-mail address and create a password for their account. Alternately, new users can set up an account linked to their Facebook or Google account. Once you have an account, you can create pinboards and add pinned images to them. It is easiest to start browsing for images on Pinterest, since so much is there. However, it is also helpful to add the Pinterest Pin button to your internet browser. The Pin button can be added to Chrome, Firefox, or Microsoft Edge. Pinterest may ask you if you want to install the button when you open your account. If it doesn't, or you want to add it after the fact, first make sure you are using one of the accepted browsers. Next, you can go directly to the browser button install page at about.pinterest.com/browser-button.[5] You can also search Help for "browser button" by clicking on the menu dots at the top of the screen and choosing Get Help. Having the button in a browser allows users to pin images from almost any website. You can also search or browse Pinterest easily using the search bar at the top or clicking the Pinterest P icon to go to the Home screen.

Each Pinterest user has a personal profile that they can update as often as they wish. The profile consists of a name, user image, a short bio, username address, and location. A blog or website can also be linked to the account. Users can update their profile information when they first create their account and afterward by clicking on their name or user image and clicking either the bolt icon (on mobile; see figure 10.2) or the pencil icon (in a browser; see figure 10.3). Pinners can choose a username that automatically turns into a Pinterest web address with the username at the end: www.pinterest.com/username. The username can be changed later, but that also changes the address. For that reason, it is recommended to not change your username often. Pinterest profiles also contain a list of the pinner's boards. If boards are secret, then only the owner will see the boards listed in their profile.

Once an account and profile are created, pinners can create or browse. To create a new pinboard, users can

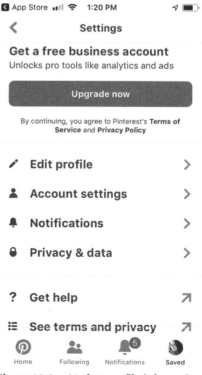

Figure 10.2.   Update profile information using the Pinterest mobile app.

Figure 10.3. Update profile information using Pinterest on a computer.

click on their name or user image and click on the +. Users can see all of their pinboards in their profile at any time and can edit them by clicking on the pencil icon that appears next to the board name when you mouse over or click on the board name. In the board Edit menu, users can change the name of the board, the board description, and the category. This is also where the Secret / Not Secret board setting can be turned on or off. Board creators can also invite other people to be collaborators on a board, which is a wonderful feature for people working on a project together, such as an anniversary party or a new home. Collaborators can be found by their Pinterest name or invited using an e-mail address. Once a board exists users can search for items to pin to it on Pinterest or the web, using the Pin button. Users can also upload one of their own images by using the same + icon to create boards and choosing Upload. To do this from a mobile phone, users will need to allow access to their photos from the mobile app.

If a new user is not ready to create a board or does not want to, they can browse or search for keywords and choose who they want to follow. Clicking on any Pinterest image will show the image larger; it also will show information about the pin, including the user and the board they posted the image to. To follow the user or the board, click on it and look for a big red button marked "Follow." You can see and change what you follow at any time by clicking on Following in either the browser or the mobile app. You can also click on Home to see boards and people that you follow, as well as suggested pins and pinners.

Pinners using an internet browser on a computer can find most settings, including the Get Help menu, terms and privacy, and account notifications by clicking on the three-dot icon (see figure 10.4). The same details on the mobile app can be found by clicking on the profile image and choosing the bolt icon in the upper right.

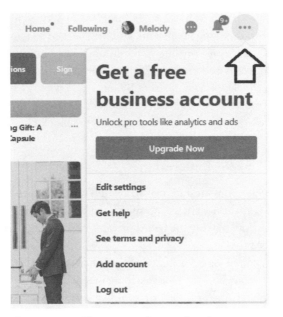

Figure 10.4.   Pinterest settings and options.

The other prominent and useful icon in both the app and the browser version of Pinterest is the notifications, which appears as a bell icon. Pinners can click on this to see activity on Pinterest, such as who is pinning and re-pinning their images. This is also a place where Pinterest will share boards similar to the user's boards so they can find new things to follow and re-pin.

PRIVACY AND SAFETY

Pinterest is relatively safe in comparison with other social networks because most of the images posted to a person's board are usually not created by that person. That means it is less likely that someone can tell where you live or work based on the images that you post and cannot find out personal information about you as easily.

Pinterest does not allow sexually explicit images or nudity, making it safer for family use compared to many other social networks. Keep in mind, though, that Pinterest's terms of use require users to be 13 years old to create an account. If an image does appear that violates this rule, it can be reported by clicking on the three-dot menu and select Report Pin.

Pinterest allows users to block other profiles. Blocking prevents someone from following or messaging the person, and the blocked account can no longer interact with the user's pins (including re-pinning, commenting, etc.). To block a user, go to that user's account by either searching for them or clicking on their name. Click on the flag icon and select Block. Users who are blocked will not receive a notification that they have been blocked. However, they will be alerted if they try to interact with pins or the account of the blocking user.

Some Safety Tips for Pinterest

- If you are using Pinterest to plan an event (like a wedding or birthday) and the board contains locations and specific information (like the date of your event), consider making the board private. You can still invite friends and family to see the board.
- Create a separate login for Pinterest when creating an account, rather than linking it to Facebook or Google. Remember, the more accounts that are linked together, the greater the risk if just one of the linked accounts experiences a data breach.
- You are not required to use a full or real name on Pinterest, even though many users do. If you are using Pinterest for personal projects and do not care whether other users can easily find you, then using a partial or fake name is a way to stay private.

SPECIAL FEATURES

Picked for You pins are the images that Pinterest suggests to you based on your pinning and other activity on the network. You will see those pins mixed with pins from boards and people you follow when you view the Home screen. If you would prefer to only see boards and people that you follow, you can hide Picked for You pins on your Following tab. You can also hide individual Picked for You pins that you do not like to help Pinterest know what it should suggest to you in the future. To do that, click on the three-dot menu and click Hide on any pin.

Visual Search is an option that allows users to find images visually similar to a pinned image. To use visual search, click on the rounded square corners icon in the lower right of any pin. The results will include similar images, as well as common subject keywords used for those images. This feature can be helpful for finding memes that all use the same image but use different text.

OTHER NOTABLE
SOCIAL MEDIA
PLATFORMS

There are more than a few giant social media platforms, but there are hundreds of smaller or niche social sites out there. New social media platforms show up all the time, and some don't last very long. Others are so specific that you may never hear about them if they are not tailored to your interests. For example, Ravelry.com is a social site where people who crochet and knit can share patterns, ideas, and projects. BizSugar is a social media site just for business owners. And there are many, many more. Some social media like WeChat, QQ, and QZone are much more popular in China and other non-English-speaking countries. Each of those platforms is currently more popular than Twitter or Reddit in China but have less of a following in the United States.

While you cannot know (or be part of) every social media network, being aware of networks that fit your interests can be enjoyable. This chapter reviews some of the smaller but interesting social media networks. It also looks at tips and basic information about different kinds of social media, including dating networks, genealogy and DNA sharing networks, and messaging apps. No matter which social media you decide to use, don't forget to review the basic tools and suggestions for all social media outlined in chapter 1.

NEXTDOOR

Nextdoor (nextdoor.com) is a locally focused social network that connects people who live in the same neighborhood or region. It is a way for neighbors to communicate about area concerns and questions. Individuals cannot join without address verification. Verifying your address can be done by requesting a postcard with a verification code, adding a phone number that is billed using your home address, or using credit or debit card verification. For credit or debit, Nextdoor checks the address but does not charge the credit card or store the information.[1]

If you are not sure about most social networks, you may still enjoy Nextdoor because of its hyper-local focus. Neighbors report all manner of things, including local events that will affect traffic in the neighborhood; garage sales; crime or problems in the area; free items to give away; lost and found pets; and questions and recommendations for lawn or home care. Because you must verify your address to become a member of your specific neighborhood, there should not be people from outside the area on your Nextdoor page trying to sell things—if there are, you can report them to the site. Despite it being mainly your neighbors, some non-neighbors (mainly organizations) will have access. Many cities have integrated school and police information with Nextdoor so that they can not only monitor complaints and issues but also share community information with people in a specific area.

Privacy risks on Nextdoor are a little different than many social networks because the people who interact with one another on the site all live close together. When you post photos or information about yourself on Nextdoor, there is a very real possibility that people will know who you are because they live nearby. They may recognize a car or home if you have them in your photos. Be safe when corresponding with neighbors, especially if you choose to meet with someone live to buy or sell an item. Bring someone with you to any such transaction and do not respond if people are pushy or act strangely. If you are ever threatened or in danger, do not report the incident to Nextdoor but to your local police instead.

It also helps to review your sharing settings on Nextdoor. One of the first things to do is to turn off exact address sharing, which tells others your specific address. To change this to just your street name, go to your profile picture then your name/profile and click on Privacy under your address. You can also "personalize" what nearby neighborhoods you want to include in your posts and view. You will always have access to your own neighborhood but may want to include additional surrounding neighborhoods when you ask a question or respond to one. When you add a post, you will have the option to choose the neighborhoods you want to include (see figure 11.1). You can select your immediate neighborhood, all nearby neighborhoods, or you can customize

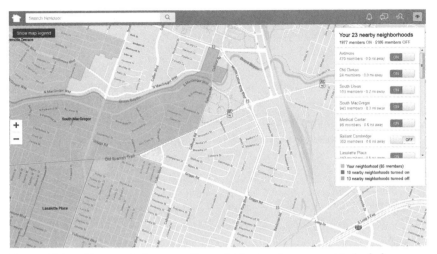

Figure 11.1. Choose what surrounding neighborhoods you want to include.

to select only certain areas. You can also adjust your neighbor preferences by searching the Help screen for "Nearby Neighborhoods preferences page" and following instructions, which are different depending on whether you are using a computer, iPhone, or Android device.

DATING NETWORKS

The Economist reports that one-sixth of American first meetings that end up in marriage start with a dating website or app.[2] There are entire books written about online dating, and each app and website has its own account management and privacy challenges. Tinder, Match, eHarmony, Christian Mingle, and OkCupid (to name just a few) are definitely social media networks, but they are different than Facebook or Twitter because of their very specific purpose. If you are using online dating networks, do some initial research about which sites make sense for you based on your interests and the cost of any services. Once you have narrowed down your options, search for the site name and "reviews" and then separately for "privacy" to get more information. Yes, the point of these sites is to find someone with whom you will connect and share lots of personal information. But until you are ready, share less to avoid becoming the target of scammers and people who will ultimately be crossed off your list of interests.

No matter which network you choose, there are some basic privacy and safety concerns that will help you when online dating. Here are some considerations to get you started:

- Use the right network. Tinder, for example, is for people who want to meet other people who are close by. That encourages quick in-person meetings. It may also make it easier to leave after meeting (if you want to) since you have not shared much information. Some dating sites have more structure or encourage longer periods of communication before meeting. Some even facilitate chaperones or group dates. Others, like Jdate and FarmersOnly, are meant for specific audiences (see figure 11.2). Don't just use what a friend suggests. Doing your research into the best network for you will make your experience better and safer.
- Balance your profile details. You want to offer enough information for others to get to know you, but you don't want to offer so much that they can tell who you are by Googling overly specific details.
- Never give out private details like your social security number, bank account number, or credit card numbers to someone you meet online. Most dating sites have strict rules prohibiting asking for money or donations, and people who do it should be reported.
- Create unique accounts for online dating instead of using your Facebook or Google account to log in. Yes, it is easier to use those logins and not create new passwords. But if there is ever a data breach to any of the related companies your data will be safer if the accounts are not linked.

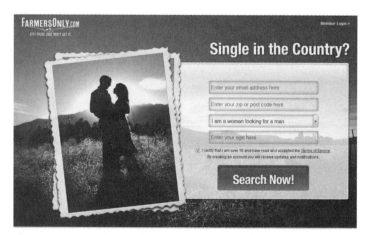

Figure 11.2.   FarmersOnly.com caters to a specific audience.

- Look for safety features on your chosen site. Match, the largest online dating network, allows users to selectively hide or make their profile visible to specific other members, allowing for a more private search (note that this option is an upcharge service). Investigate and browse account settings on your chosen platform to make the most of them.
- Don't provide personal contact information too soon. Share through the app or site until you are sure you want the person to know who and where you are. Sharing your phone number, address, e-mail, and social media accounts too quickly puts you at risk to people who may not be serious.
- Do not send photos by text or e-mail unless you have stripped out location information from the photos' metadata. If you don't know how to do that, there are many tutorials available online. If you don't strip out the location, then you will be sharing the geographic coordinates of where the photo was taken with the person who receives it. If the photo was taken in your home or where you work, then you are sharing those locations. Dating networks usually strip out that information when you post photos in your account, which is safer. Be in control and only share what you mean to share.

Online Dating Network Terminology

Catfishing—When someone is pretending to be someone they are not, they are said to be *catfishing* you. For example, they say they are a much younger, more successful person but are not being honest. Usually these people will only agree to talk online and never meet in person.

Ghosting—This term describes the situation when someone you have been talking with or dating completely and abruptly cuts off all communication without any explanation.

Sliding into DMs / DM Slide—DM is short for direct messages. *Sliding into my DMs* refers to the act of someone you only know online taking the "next step" to privately chat with you. Often you only know the person on social media or from a dating site and then social media.

Swiping (Left or Right)—This refers to the functionality of many online dating networks (including Tinder, Bumble, and more) that allows people to see a photo of a potential match and swipe based on interest/attraction: swiping right for interest and swiping left to move on. If both people swipe right, they can connect since both are interested.

GENEALOGY AND DNA NETWORKS

Genealogy networks like Family.me and Ancestry.com, as well as DNA sharing sites like 23andMe.com are currently very popular and can be used to connect with known family, find more distant family members, and chat with people researching family history in the same geographic areas. What used to be a lone research task in the archives is now full of social, online connection and information sharing. With the recent popularity of DNA testing, distant relatives are finding one another more and more often. Each family-focused network offers different features, and many are paid networks because of online access to database resources. For DNA sites like 23andMe, you must purchase and send in a DNA test to participate.

People use genealogy sites like Ancestry.com for a variety of reasons. Many have free tools like charts and tutorials. Others have additional access and services with paid subscriptions. With Ancestry, you can use the site to search for resources and build family trees without connecting to other people. However, some of the resources are shared by others who use the site.[3] You may find a photograph and a family tree that interacts with yours (such as through a marriage), and most genealogists and family historians cannot resist reaching out to find out more from a family connection. Often the site suggests a person who has a family tree or DNA match, and you can send them a direct message through the site. Some sites, including Ancestry, allow you to search for site users by their name or username (see figure 11.3).

With DNA sites, many users are hoping to fill in gaps in their family history. Not all people using DNA test sites are interested in genealogy. They might be looking for adopted or lost relatives, or they may be curious about their familial origin. In any case, people on DNA-only sites tend to be slightly different in focus to genealogy researchers. Because of the collaborative nature of genealogy research, it is common for family historians and genealogists to reach out to one another when they see their information overlap. However, DNA test participants may not be interested in connecting, even with relatives. As with any social network, people will each choose how they will use a site and with whom they want to connect. There is no "right" way, and you should not be offended if someone you want to connect to on a genealogy site does not respond to your requests.

Those using genealogy and DNA networks should consider downloading their data. Unlike some social media networks, genealogy and DNA data has very personal details, many of which might have taken a lot of time and effort to compile. Losing that data can be awful, especially since it is usually possible to preserve it. DNA data can often be downloaded in raw file formats, or in a PDF

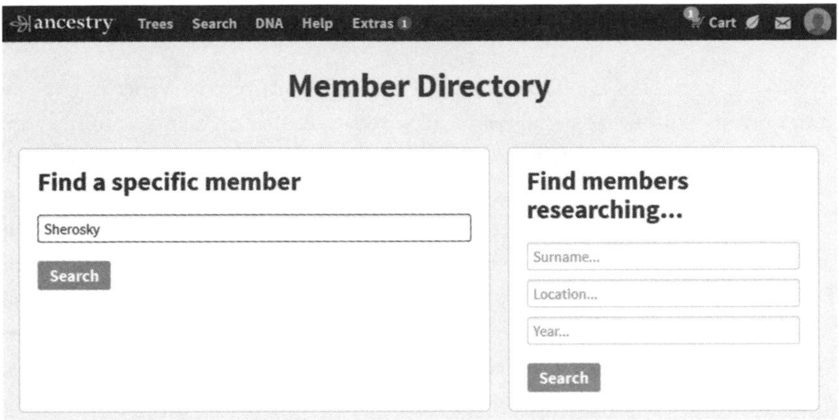

Figure 11.3. Ancestry user search.

report.[4] Some people feel uncomfortable having their DNA information on the web and may wish to download their data and erase their information from the vendor website; most of the vendors allow you to do this and claim to delete all copies of your DNA information at your request. For genealogy data, like family trees and relationships, GEDCOM is the preferred file format. GEDCOM can be exported and imported into almost all genealogy software and is the best option for saving your genealogy data when switching systems.

Some privacy tips for genealogy networks:

- Be careful with information about the living. Living people, especially children, should be protected from online identification and identity theft by limiting how much personal information is available about them online. Remember, security questions for many online accounts ask the same sorts of information that people share on genealogy sites.
- Check your public-facing view. Ancestry offers a See Public View menu option in profile account settings. If the site you are using does not offer that, ask a friend if you can use their computer to search for your account. Make sure that you are comfortable with anything that is visible publicly on the internet and remove anything that you don't want to be shared that widely. Some sites may additionally offer preferences that hide the information or any public view.
- Be cautious when connecting to DNA relatives. They are family, but if you have not met them, they are also still strangers. Be cautious when meeting anyone in real life that you connected with online, even if they are related to you.

SKYPE, WHATSAPP, AND OTHER MESSAGING APPS

Messaging networks including Skype, Line, WhatsApp, and Viber overlap in functionality with other social media networks that offer chat and a mobile app. Most of these apps provide small-group or one-on-one communication through mobile apps as their primary focus. People use messaging apps for a variety or reasons, ranging from preference to function. Often they use them because others they communicate with prefer them, which makes some more or less used by region or group. Most messaging apps will work with a Wi-fi network even when a phone has no service, making it possible to chat and call even when someone is out of network, traveling internationally, or just out of minutes. Privacy is also a factor in why some people might use a mobile app over their built-in SMS option. Messaging apps each have their own privacy setup and are generally considered to be more secure that messaging through your phone's built-in apps. The original creators of WhatsApp, for example, have named privacy as one of their core principles for designing it.[5] WhatsApp and Signal have become popular for security features including disappearing messages and end-to-end encryption.[6]

Privacy on messaging apps varies, and some apps offer more options than others. Here are some privacy and security issues to consider when using messaging apps:

- Choose a messaging app with encryption.
- Compare privacy and security at Secure Messaging App Comparison: https://www.securemessagingapps.com/. This site looks at multiple messaging apps in chart form and asks security and privacy questions including, "Surveillance capability built into the app?" and "App collects customers' data?"[7]
- Just because it is encrypted and more secure than other media does not mean you can say anything. Just like any other communication, it may be intercepted, shared by the message's receiver, or be subject to a data breach. While this is unlikely, regularly there are news stories outlining "secure" communication that was unintentionally shared.[8]

SOME FINAL NICHE AND NOTABLE NETWORKS TO CHECK OUT

4chan (4chan.org) is an anonymous, English-language image and comment posting website where the most recent posts appear at the top. The site is split up into individual boards that each have their own guidelines and focus. However, the random board "/b/" is the most popular.[9] Memes (sharable, often comedic images) are often born on 4chan before being shared on other social media networks like Reddit or Twitter. Because it is anonymous, 4chan is known to be chaotic. Anyone can access the site by simply accepting the disclaimer that they are not a minor (as some content is adult in nature). Proponents of the site love that they will see new internet news, images, and video first before other networks. Critics find the random and often offensive comments and posts to be off-putting or confusing.

Flickr (Flickr.com) is an image- and video-hosting site owned by SmugMug where users can store and share content. It is popular with both professional and hobby photographers. Photographers can set up profiles where they create public and private photo and video galleries. You must have an account to upload content but do not need to be an account holder to see posted media on Flickr. You must also have an account to connect to other people as contacts on the site. Free accounts are limited to 1,000 photos or videos, or you can upgrade to Flickr Pro to get unlimited storage. Flickr users can comment on one another's photographs and discuss photography and related topics (such as software, equipment, locations, and more) in Flickr groups.

Goodreads (goodreads.com) is a social network for readers and book lovers. Users can track the books they are reading and books they want to read. They can also connect with friends, share book recommendations, and write reviews. Goodreaders can set an annual reading goal and congratulate one another on reaching their reading count each year. Authors can additionally create an author page where they can interact with people who have read (or want to read) their books. Goodreads is owned by Amazon.com, allowing it to keep book and author information up to date, even with new releases. The site is free.

Meetup.com is a free online network for connecting people in real life through shared interests. People can join Meetup.com to browse or create real-life meetups to do just about anything. Topics vary widely and may include beekeeping groups, board game get-togethers, new language learners, or people who want to go out line dancing together. Events are organized geographically, so you can search for things that are happening in your area. On the site, you can add a profile image and biographical information, including interests. You can also join meetup groups to get announcements about upcoming group events. Meetup.com is popular with people who are new to an area, looking to make new friends, or want to learn new skills.

NaNoWriMo (nanowrimo.org) is a social network and nonprofit devoted to helping people write a novel during National Novel Writing Month each

November. NaNoWriMo does not describe itself as a social network. However, it is a place where thousands of people with a common purpose come together to communicate. While the primary focus is during the November writing challenge, the site is active all year and hosts a variety of activities. Users share story ideas, connect with others locally and virtually, and track progress on writing and editing projects. Writers can create profiles where they can add an avatar and other media, like draft book covers for their writing projects. The site is free but encourages donations to help the nonprofit continue.

Ravelry is a knit and crochet community launched in 2007 for people who enjoy fiber arts. Members can share projects and ideas on the site, which also features a database of patterns. Fiber artists can create their own profile page with biographic information, knitting and crocheting background, and photos of their arts projects. Users can find one another to chat and connect, or chat through groups, which are forums on specific topics. Knitters can even find out about specific yarns, since "each yarn has its own page on Ravelry." Yarn pages offer information about each yarn and example projects that people have made from them (see figure 11.4).

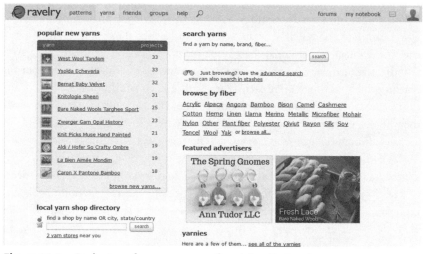

Figure 11.4. Projects and yarn pages on the niche site Ravelry.com.

ARCHIVING, SAVING, AND LEGACY MANAGEMENT

Once you learn to survive social media and manage your accounts, you may find yourself creating things on social media that you don't want to lose. Can you save things that you post on social media? Can you save things that other people post? Can other people save things you posted or created? What happens when we close our accounts or pass away? Does all of that information disappear, or it is out there on the internet forever? What if we want to capture some portion of it and pass it on to someone else? These are not easy questions. This chapter will look at how to save and archive social media so that you can protect your own data into the future.

ONCE IT'S ON THE INTERNET, IT'S THERE FOREVER, RIGHT?

Many of us have heard this: once it is on the internet, it is "out there" somewhere forever. This is not exactly true. It is definitely possible to lose things that you post on the internet. There is no one place that stores and preserves everything. Social media is a special case, too, since usually users have to log in to see their connections and posted information. That means that, unless the social media site or a parent company with access decides to preserve the data, outside groups like Internet Archive, libraries, or individuals can only do so much. In many cases, individuals can seek to preserve their own posts and information, and they can usually capture some of the things that their friends and connections post. Since many people don't think about this, though, there is a lot of likely data lost when a social media company disappears or merges with another company.

REASONS TO ARCHIVE OR SAVE

Many people want to save social media posts to keep a record of online interactions with friends and family. It is the digital equivalent of saving letters and postcards. Someone may want to preserve an online chat with a loved one who has passed away. They may want to save photos that they posted from a phone that got lost and was not backed up. Social media may be the only place where people posted comments and well wishes after the birth of your child or congratulations after you announce your new job. It is natural to want to save some of that correspondence.

You may want the data. We spend so much time online that you may want to download your social media information to get a better picture of your online life. Most of the major social media sites allow you to download what you have posted as well as the details and information that they have collected about you. It can be interesting to see what Facebook thinks you like and what should be advertised to you. Combining your posts and news from multiple online accounts may additionally give you perspective into your personal growth and history.

There may be things that other people post online that you did not create, so the only access you have is through social media. There is no original on your end because someone else posted the photo or news. Unfortunately, depending on what was posted, you may or may not have easy access to this sort of information. There are many challenges to this issue. For example, what if a loved one passes away and you want to save photos that they posted of the two of you together? There are some options for saving things like this. In general, however, if there are rules in place that prevent access to other people's posts and information, their privacy should be respected. Most social media accounts will not let you save other people's posts and comments with their archiving tools.

WHAT SAVING IS *NOT*

Saving your social media is not a backup. You should plan to download any social media data that you want to preserve and also back up your computer to protect yourself from loss, like hardware failure, disaster, or theft. Social media accounts may choose to change their rules at any time: every user agreement allows them to change things with little to no liability related to the losses of their users. The photo-sharing site Flickr recently decided in 2018 that they would limit free storage and delete all photos over that limit for nonpaying accounts.[1] If you used Flickr years ago and did not pay attention to this change, you may have lost photos during the change. Ideally, you have any of your online accounts and files saved *and* backed up outside of the social media site itself.

Saving things from social media is also not a replacement for preserving the originals. Social media accounts often reduce file size and strip out metadata, like location, from your images. Why does that matter? If you ever want to print the image or sort it using photo software that uses that location metadata, you can't replace the original with a lower-quality shot. In other words, don't plan to post to social media, delete the original, and back up the social media image later. Facebook and Instagram are not storage; they are built for sharing, not saving.

HOW TO ARCHIVE

There are some very basic ways to save a single image or small portion of your social media. Each of these methods has benefits and drawbacks, but they are easy for people who do not want to use more advanced technology tools. Basic tools include screenshots, print to PDF functionality, and saving pages as HTML. This chapter also covers a few aggregate tools: IFTTT, digi.me, and physical options. Each social media platform additionally comes with some tools of its own. Some are more full featured than others.

Basic Tools

Taking a screenshot is one way to capture what you see on a social media platform. You can take a screenshot using a mobile device or personal computer, and it will save an image of whatever appears on the screen at that moment in time. Since social media is dynamic and sometimes changes or moves as more people post, taking a screenshot is a quick way to capture what you are seeing. Mobile device screenshot options will vary. However, usually pressing the home or power button together with volume down will take a screenshot and save it to your phone's photo album. On an Apple computer (laptop or desktop), hold Command + Control + Shift + 4 to choose what portion of the screen should be included. The default on Apple computers is to copy the image after it is selected, so you will need to open a document or e-mail and paste the image right away. There is no built-in function for non-Apple computers, but there is a simple and free option through Dropbox that will save all screenshots in a Dropbox folder. Download Dropbox to your computer and open the program. The Dropbox icon should appear in the bar on the lower right (on a PC) or upper right (on Apple) of your screen. Right click the Dropbox icon and choose the gear icon in the pop-up window. Choose Preferences, then go to the Import tab. There is a box to check for "Share screenshots using Dropbox" (see figure 12.1). Once that is selected, PC users can click the Print Screen button (PrtScn) to save a screenshot, and Apple users can use the built-in functions on those devices. This option can also be turned on in your phone settings. That way, all screenshots from all of your devices are shared to the same folder.

Screenshots may not work for all projects. Obviously it will not work to screenshot your entire account—that would take forever. Also, screenshots turn everything into a picture. That means that none of the text from the original posts remains text. Words that appear in the image file will not be searchable

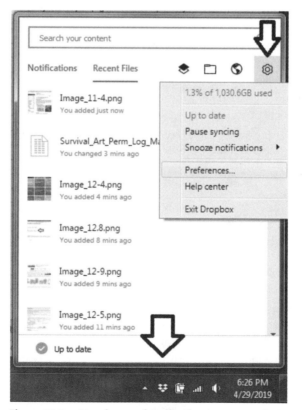

Figure 12.1.   Dropbox preferences for easy screenshots.

and cannot be copied and pasted as they might in an HTML or PDF document. Still, to capture what you see on the screen exactly as it appears, screenshots have a place in social media archiving.

Another option is to print to PDF from a computer (rather than a mobile device). To use this option, go to File and Print Preview while viewing your account on a computer. Depending on the social media platform, the print view will not look correct. Some social media is too dynamic to be captured in this way. Using Print to PDF from the Facebook news feed, for example, does not usually include most posts and images. Often clicking on a post or photo to get the full view will let you take a better PDF (see figure 12.2). That is the case for Instagram: viewed on a computer screen, Print to PDF captures individual Instagram posts and their comments with text intact. That means that the text will be searchable, and you can copy and paste it out of the resulting PDF. This method requires some trial and error and will have different results depending on the platform and post.

Save as HTML is another very basic option available for saving many web pages, including some social media. HTML means hypertext markup language. It is the standard way that web pages track the font, color, and effects of a page for display through your browser. If you are able to save an HTML file, you can open it in a web browser to see the page. If the capture is possible (and the

Figure 12.2. Capturing an individual post as PDF often has better results than trying to capture the live feed.

site is not built in too complicated of a manner), you can save the look and feel of the site that you are trying to capture. Depending on your browser and the site, there are one or more ways to save the HTML. To create an HTML file, you can go to File at the top of the browser screen or right click anywhere on the page, then choose Save Page As. HTML will be one of the file type options available. If the capture works well, the page will more or less look the same as the social media site—but it is saved locally and not on the internet. As with the Print to PDF menu option, Save as HTML options work better when you open a specific post to save. Trying to capture a feed, such as your Facebook news feed or never-ending Twitter feed, will not work since that data is constantly refreshed and changing dynamically. Save as HTML works well for Tumblr posts and LinkedIn profiles. Once saved as an HTML file, computers with Adobe can convert the files to PDF.

External Options

Only a few highly functional aggregate tools exist for individuals who want to archive multiple social media platforms. Digi.me and IFTTT are two of those tools. Since technology options are steadily growing and there is a strong interest in saving social media, it is likely there will be more practical options in the future. In all cases, remember that you should not share your social media passwords and access with just anyone. If a company is still relatively new, it is safer to wait until it has been reviewed by technology blogs. Tools that are useful and become popular are commonly vetted by online sources and criticized for any security risks. Read reviews and do not give access to your accounts unless you feel comfortable with the reputability of the company involved.

Digi.me (https://digi.me/) is a company that offers tools for social media and personal data aggregating.[2] Digi.me allows users to download, sort, and store their own data from multiple accounts. The company does not store or save your data: they just work as a go-between to aggregate all of the information from multiple sources into one place. Once combined, you can sort by date, search by keyword, and export all or part of your information (see figure 12.3). The application is free for mobile devices and computers, though the computer program has more export options. Currently, it is the most full-featured social media archiving tool available to individuals.

IFTTT stands for "If This, Then That." IFTTT (https://ifttt.com/) is a free site that helps you create workflows (called Applets) between multiple accounts or tools. IFTTT offers several prebuilt applets that you can use to archive your accounts the way you want them. For example, applets already exist that can back up your Pinterest pins to your Google Drive account. To make it work, you have to give IFTTT access to the related accounts. Then, once it is turned on, the process happens automatically. You can continue to use Pinterest normally and go to Google Drive any time to see your Pinterest pin archive. You can go to IFTTT to turn off the applet. IFTTT can connect to all major social media networks and many other technology tools and services, including Dropbox, Twitter, WordPress, Instagram, and e-mail services. It has a whole section devoted to applets for social media, and many of those are related to saving or sharing between platforms (see figure 12.4). It is a free tool to explore, especially if none of the other options meet your archiving needs.

As weird as it sounds, saving social media in a physical format is also

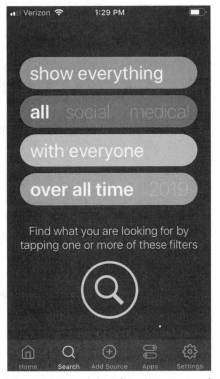

Figure 12.3. Digi.me has many sort and save options.

an option. Multiple online stores allow you to print a book using images and posts from your social media account. Mysocialbook.com offers this service for Facebook and Instagram. Chatbooks and Shutterfly offer similar options. TweetBookz will do the same for Twitter. Tumblr and other blogs can be printed by intorealpages.com, BlookUp, or many similar sites. While this is not as secure as a digital archive, creating a print copy is a nice way to have extra copies of your online life.

Built-In Platform Tools

Many social media networks have built-in functionality that lets you save things from the site. Most of the major platforms' download and archive options are described in this chapter. YouTube also provides video tutorials for many of these methods. Each platform's options vary widely and may let you capture only certain parts of your social media interactions. In particular, most plat-

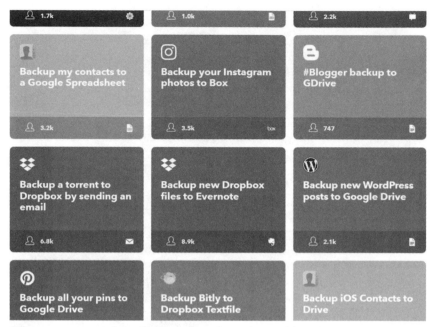

Figure 12.4. IFTTT has multiple applets for saving social media posts.

forms do not have a way to capture the comments and responses that other people add to your posts. This is due to privacy concerns: you have long-term access to your own posts and comments, since you created them. But other people's comments are their own, and social media platforms usually only allow access to your own personal comments and posts. Missing reactions are one of the largest gaps in what you can save from social media using built-in tools. If you want to save these sorts of comments, consider using screenshots or investigating more advanced web-archiving tools.

Facebook

Facebook has a built-in archive function that allows you to download both your Facebook data, as well as data that Facebook has collected about you. The process is fairly straightforward and is now available via the web version as well as the mobile app. On a computer (Mac or PC), log in to your account and click on the tiny down arrow in the upper right and go to Settings. Choose the Your Facebook Information option from the menu on the left. You will see an option called Download Your Information and can click on View to get to the Download menu. On the app, click on the three-line menu > Settings and Privacy > Account Settings > Your Facebook Information > Download Your Information.

The provided options are quite extensive and are basically the same on mobile and computer (see figure 12.5). You can include or exclude the information that you want by clicking on the blue checkmark next to the information. Possible options include archiving all of your posts, photos and videos, Messenger chats, profile information, and topics you enjoy that Facebook has gathered about you for advertising purposes. You can download data from a specific date range or for your entire account history. You also have the option to download high, medium, or low-quality media. Keep in mind that your media may have been reduced in size when you first uploaded it; Facebook's options for this have changed over the years as to how much they reduce file size and quality for web viewing. If you are creating an archival copy and may not have other copies of the images, choose high media quality. File type options include HTML, which can be opened in an internet browser, or JSON (Java Script Object Notification) file, which is a more data-focused download.

Once you decide what data you want to include and click on Create File, Facebook will start compiling the file for download. Depending on how much information you included this may take a while. Once it is done, the file will

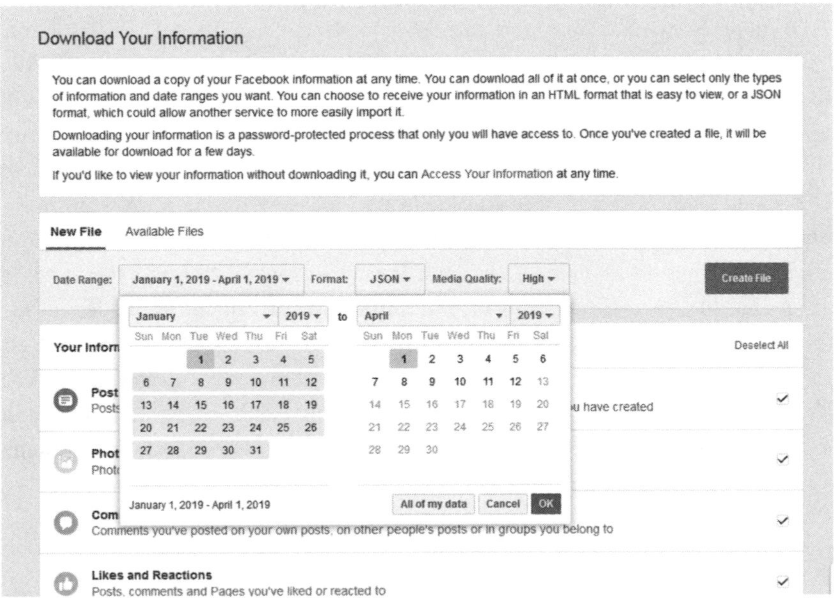

Figure 12.5. Facebook "Download Your Information" options.

appear in the Available Files tab. Click the button next to the search results to download. You can create multiple different searches for your data if you want it to be separated for some reason. Once downloaded, you will have a copy of your information saved offline, where you can back it up as an archive or just look back at it for fun. HTML files will allow you to see a visual representation of your data, which will look something like your Facebook's interface. JSON is more data focused, and those files can be used to pull into other programs to collate or sort your data. If you download an HTML file, you can drag the file into an internet browser (like Chrome or Firefox) to see your archive. JSON files can be converted into CSV and viewed in an Excel file if you wanted to be able to sort your friend list or organize your Facebook posts.

Instagram

Instagram has a built-in function that allows users to download their photos and other information.[3] Though Instagram is owned by Facebook, you do not get as many options to choose from when downloading your Instagram account. The download that is created will include your photos, comments you have made, and profile information. Since there are not many options to choose from, the process is straightforward. However, you can only have one archive compiling at a time. Though Instagram is mainly a mobile app, you can also log in to your account on a personal computer and download your data there. Log in to your account on a computer and click on the gear icon next to your username. Select the Privacy and Security menu option and scroll down to Data Download. On the app, click on the little person icon, then the three-line menu in the upper right. Choose Settings (gear icon) from the menu, then Privacy and Security > Download Data. You will need to type in your password to confirm your identity. Once you request your data, Instagram will e-mail you a link to follow to retrieve your information for download. It may take up to 48 hours to assemble your data, and once created the link and download will only be available for four days (see figure 12.6). The resulting file download will be a ZIP file folder. You can open the ZIP file to unpack media files like photos and images, as well as JSON files that contain your non-media text data. You can open the JSON file in a text editor or convert it to CSV and view in spreadsheet form to see comments and other text-specific Instagram details.

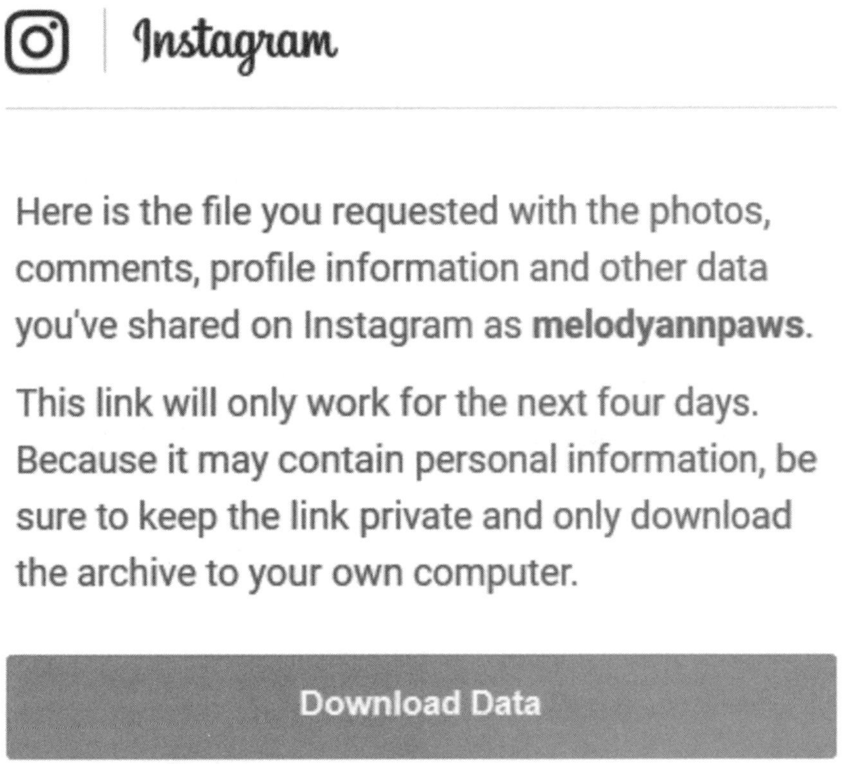

| *Instagram*

Here is the file you requested with the photos, comments, profile information and other data you've shared on Instagram as **melodyannpaws**.

This link will only work for the next four days. Because it may contain personal information, be sure to keep the link private and only download the archive to your own computer.

Download Data

Figure 12.6. Instagram will send a link for archive download.

LinkedIn

LinkedIn offers built-in functions for exporting your account details and contacts from the site. It also offers a quick PDF download of your profile. For a profile PDF, simply go to your profile (click Me > View Profile) and click on More under your profile image and title. Your profile in PDF will immediately be available for viewing or saving. For other account download options, click on the Me menu option or your profile image in the top bar to get to the Account menu. Click Settings and Privacy and scroll down to the How LinkedIn Uses Your Data menu option. Click on Change to see the Download menu (see figure 12.7). You can either choose to download everything that is offered or choose individual files, including articles, imported contacts, recommendations, connections, messages, and more. Once choices are selected you must type in your password to confirm you are the account holder. The download may not be ready for up to 24 hours depending on how much you included in the request. When it is finished, LinkedIn will e-mail you a link that will lead to your downloadable files. Click on the Download Archive button to save your information as a ZIP file. Depending on what you have requested, you may get different types of file formats, including HTML and CSV (which can be opened in Excel). LinkedIn additionally offers information in its online Help Center to help you choose what data to export using its built-in tools. A link to this help option is conveniently available next to where you choose what data to include in your archive.

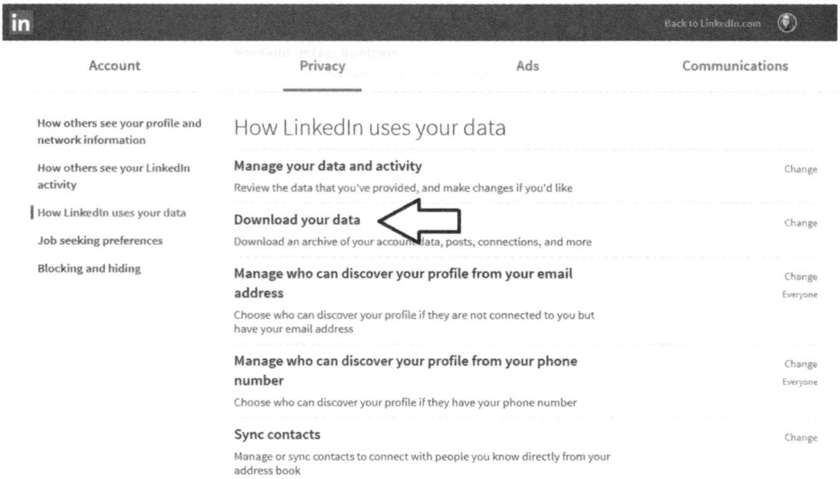

Figure 12.7. LinkedIn download option.

Pinterest

Pinterest has an option called Archive that is for saving and hiding a board for later use on the Pinterest platform: it does not allow you to create a file for download. Because it is still saved on Pinterest and cannot be backed up it likely does not meet the needs of people who truly want an archive of their Pinterest boards. Because Pinterest is made up of "pins" that belong to other people (and so likely protected by copyright), it is unlikely that they will create a tool for downloading and saving boards any time soon. However, there is a third-party app/service called Pin4Ever, available from pin4ever.com. You must provide to Pin4Ever your Pinterest login. With the app, users can download a full version of the Pinterest boards, including HTML files for each board that can be viewed through any browser. Though it is a paid service, the first archive is free. This makes it especially suitable for someone who is leaving the platform and wants to archive all their boards before closing their account. A subscription for continual archiving starts at around $2 a month. Pinners who devote a lot of time to their boards and enjoy the functionality of having origin links and pins saved to their computer outside of the platform may find enough value in the service to subscribe.

Reddit

Because Reddit posts are public, numerous, and very active, there are pros and cons for archiving. Reddit's message board format makes it difficult to capture while a discussion is in progress because comments rise and fall in the ranking order and people continue to add comments to live posts. However, after six months comments and posts are automatically archived by Reddit (see figure 12.8). Sometimes administrators lock and archive them sooner. This may meet your needs for archiving, if you just want to be able to look back at a thread or specific posts. An archived thread on Reddit means it is no longer active and cannot receive comments or be voted up or down. The thread is online and available for reading into the foreseeable future. You should be able to access any archived thread at its original subreddit web address, as long as Reddit is still up and running and does not change its policies on keeping these archived threads. Also keep in mind that links and external content may no longer work if they were hosted off-site; this is an issue with archiving web content.

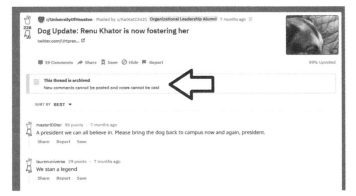

Figure 12.8. After six months, comments and posts are archived by Reddit.

For threads that are voluminous and fast changing, the archive function may not capture exactly what you want. If it does not capture the specific time or interchange that you wanted, you can also look at a certain point in time using Internet Archive's Wayback Machine. Go to http://web.archive.org/ and search for the subreddit web address (see figure 12.9). Depending on how long the subreddit has been around, you may see options for viewing the page going back for years. These are point-in-time web captures, so they will show what the thread looked like at the day and time in question. Note that not all days are available, and some content and links may not appear correctly.

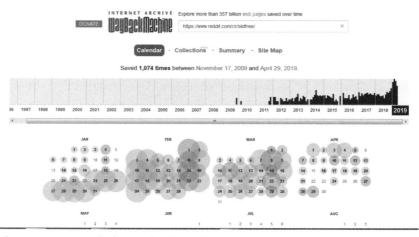

Figure 12.9. Search the Wayback Machine for old Reddit views.

If you want to save a copy of a point in time on Reddit and waiting for the archiving functionality does not work for you, there are other options. Common web archiving and save options apply. You can screenshot what you are seeing on your screen. You can print screen to PDF. You can also save the page as HTML. These options are described later in this chapter. For those with more advanced coding skills, github.com and other online code share depositories offer multiple options for Reddit archiving.[4]

Snapchat

Snapchat allows users to download their own data with a built-in Download My Data option. You must have a verified e-mail address in your account to use this function. To access this option, click on your Bitmoji/avatar and click on the gear icon to get to Settings. Scroll down to My Data and click on it. Snapchat will ask for your login information to verify your identity. Once you have verified, Snapchat offers two options for download. Some information can be viewed in the Snapchat app (see figure 12.10). For the bulk of the data, however, Snapchat will send an e-mail to the account address. Though Snapchat is a mobile app, the data file received by e-mail will be best viewed on a personal computer. The file, which will be a compressed ZIP file, includes all the information you have provided to Snapchat, chat history, friends, location history, and settings Snapchat has applied to you for advertising and lifestyle category tracking. Snaps you sent that you did not save to memories and snaps received from others will not be available in your data download. See figure 12.11 for a full list of what is included.

Figure 12.10. Some of your download-able Snapchat data is viewable in the app.

Tumblr

Tumblr offers a straightforward export and download of your blog from the web interface (not the app). To access the export option, click on the settings icon that looks like a little person. Select the Tumblr you want to export. Clicking will take you to that blog, and there will be a new menu along the right side of the screen. Choose Edit Appearance, then scroll to the bottom of the options screen. You will see a button that says Export and the name of your blog. Tumblr creates a ZIP file with your blog contents, which sometimes takes a few minutes (depending on the size of your blog). Once it is created it can be downloaded immediately. The ZIP file will include all of your blog posts in HTML, all posted media in its uploaded format (such as JPG or MP4), and blog message conversations and posts in XML. If you have multiple blogs on Tumblr, you will need to archive each one separately.

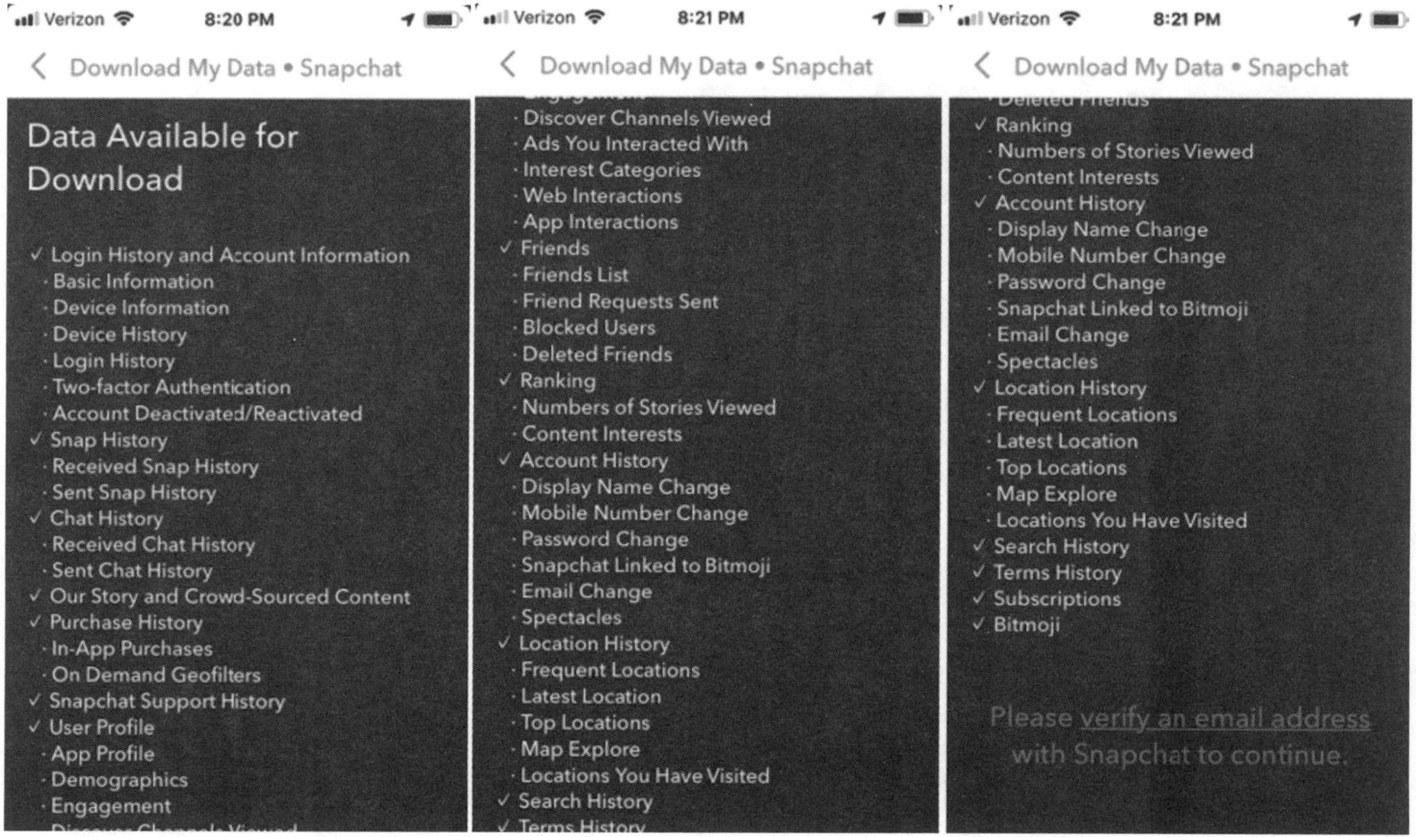

Data Available for Download

✓ Login History and Account Information
- Basic Information
- Device Information
- Device History
- Login History
- Two-factor Authentication
- Account Deactivated/Reactivated
✓ Snap History
- Received Snap History
- Sent Snap History
✓ Chat History
- Received Chat History
- Sent Chat History
✓ Our Story and Crowd-Sourced Content
✓ Purchase History
- In-App Purchases
- On Demand Geofilters
✓ Snapchat Support History
✓ User Profile
- App Profile
- Demographics
- Engagement

- Discover Channels Viewed
- Ads You Interacted With
- Interest Categories
- Web Interactions
- App Interactions
✓ Friends
- Friends List
- Friend Requests Sent
- Blocked Users
- Deleted Friends
✓ Ranking
- Numbers of Stories Viewed
- Content Interests
✓ Account History
- Display Name Change
- Mobile Number Change
- Password Change
- Snapchat Linked to Bitmoji
- Email Change
- Spectacles
✓ Location History
- Frequent Locations
- Latest Location
- Top Locations
- Map Explore
- Locations You Have Visited
- Search History
✓ Terms History

- Deleted Friends
✓ Ranking
- Numbers of Stories Viewed
- Content Interests
✓ Account History
- Display Name Change
- Mobile Number Change
- Password Change
- Snapchat Linked to Bitmoji
- Email Change
- Spectacles
✓ Location History
- Frequent Locations
- Latest Location
- Top Locations
- Map Explore
- Locations You Have Visited
✓ Search History
✓ Terms History
✓ Subscriptions
✓ Bitmoji

Please verify an email address
with Snapchat to continue.

Figure 12.11. Snapchat list of download options.

Twitter

Twitter has a built-in archival function that allows you to save your entire history of tweets. It is a basic function with few choices. To access the download function on a computer, click on your profile image in the upper right and choose Settings and Privacy. Scroll to the bottom to see a button marked Request Your Archive. Twitter will e-mail you a link when the archive is finished. When you download the ZIP file provided, start by reading the README.txt file provided by Twitter (see figure 12.12). It explains some basic information about the files included in the archive. Start with the index.html file, which can be opened in a web browser. That file will show you a visual compilation of your tweet history, including statistics of your tweets over time. The archive will also contain all of your tweets since the beginning of your account, not including tweets you have erased. Tweets will be in a CSV file, which can be opened in Google Sheets or Microsoft Excel.

Name

css

data

img

js

lib

index.html

README.txt

tweets.csv

Figure 12.12. Twitter archive's README.txt file explains your archive download.

YouTube

Saving from YouTube ranges in difficulty depending on what you want to download. If you want to download a copy of an individual video you have posted on YouTube, that process is fairly simple. Go to https://studio.youtube .com on a computer, log in to your account (if you are not already logged in), and click on the Videos option in the left-hand menu. You should see a list of the YouTube videos that you have created, including private videos. Hover your mouse button over any video and you will see a three-dot menu appear to the right of the video description (see figure 12.13). Click on the menu and choose Download. The video will download as an MP4 file, playable on most computers. If you want to download more than individual videos, you will need to go into your Google account.

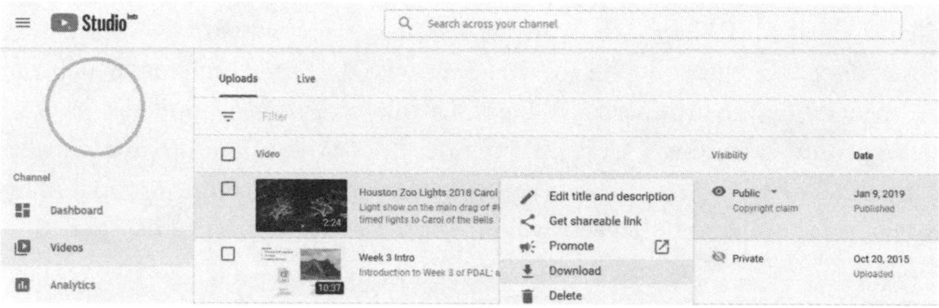

Figure 12.13.   Download any individual video from YouTube.

Downloading the bulk of your YouTube-related information is part of the Download Your Data option for all Google tools and use. To access that information, go to https://myaccount.google.com/data-and-personalization and scroll down to "Download, delete, or make a plan for your data." Click on Download Your Data to go to the extensive menu. All Google products that you can download data for are listed here, and you can select or deselect what options you want to include. YouTube is at the bottom of the list. If you only want YouTube data, choose the option at the top of the list to "Deselect All" and only check YouTube (see figure 12.14). In the YouTube section, click on the All YouTube Data Included menu option to choose what options are available for download. This includes videos, video metadata, watch and search history, comments you have added to videos, community posts, and chats. Any videos downloaded will be in their original format or in MP4 files. Other data will be in HTML or JSON. Also, as with most other built-in tools, only your own comments will be included in your download: comments other people made on your videos cannot be downloaded. After selecting your choices, you can choose how you would like the files delivered (including e-mail link or through online storage sites like Dropbox or OneDrive). Files can also be split into smaller sizes for delivery, if desired.

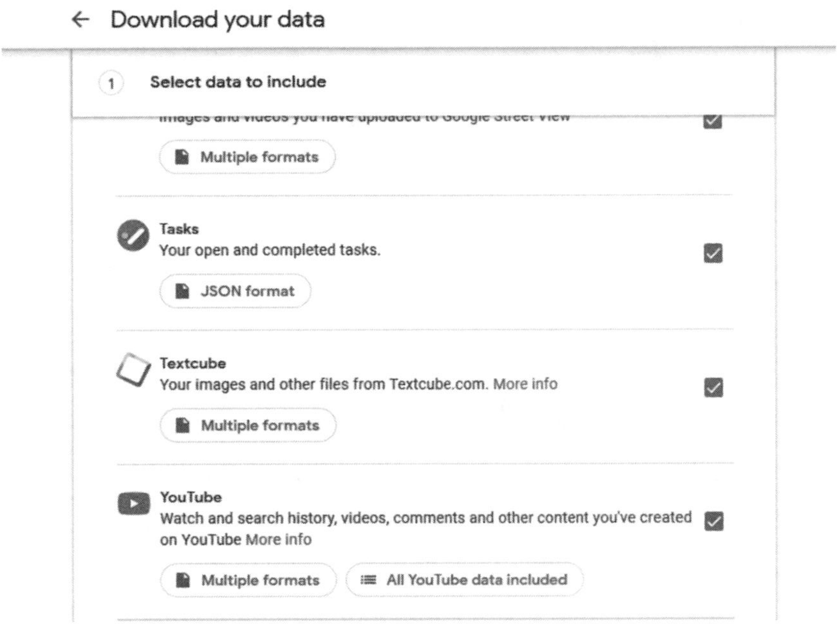

Figure 12.14. Download all YouTube details from your Google account.

FINAL THOUGHTS ON SOCIAL MEDIA ARCHIVING

There is no way to 100 percent capture social media as it looks on our mobile devices and computers. Social media is interactive and ever changing . . . it's social! That does not mean that you should not try to capture some of it. Choose the most important things in your accounts and try multiple methods to see what archiving options feel best for your purposes. Just as you cannot completely capture the day of your wedding on film, you can still remember and enjoy it with photos and video. Social media archiving can preserve memories that may otherwise be lost when a company closes. It can also help us be aware of what data exists about us out on the web. No matter your reason for archiving, trial and error will play a part as you learn about the options described in this chapter.

NOTES

PREFACE

1. "Number of Social Media Users Worldwide from 2010 to 2021 (in Billions)," *Statista*, accessed May 15, 2019, https://www.statista.com/statistics/278414/number -of-worldwide-social-network-users/.

CHAPTER 2: FACEBOOK

1. Edison Research and Triton Digital, "The Infinite Deal," March 2019, http:// www.edisonresearch.com/wp-content/uploads/2019/03/Infinite-Dial-2019-PDF-1 .pdf.

2. Matt Carlson, "Facebook in the News," *Digital Journalism* 6, no. 1 (2018): 4–20, doi: 10.1080/21670811.2017.1298044.

3. Edison Research and Triton Digital, "The Infinite Deal."

4. "What Names Are Allowed on Facebook?" Facebook Help Center, accessed March 1, 2019, https://www.facebook.com/help/112146705538576?helpref=search& sr=2&query=authentic%20name.

CHAPTER 3: TWITTER

1. Paige Cooper, "28 Twitter Statistics All Marketers Need to Know in 2018," *Hoot-suite* (blog), January 17, 2018, https://blog.hootsuite.com/twitter-statistics/.

2. "About Verified Accounts," Twitter Help, accessed November 5, 2018, https:// help.twitter.com/en/managing-your-account/about-twitter-verified-accounts.

3. "Campaign Targeting," Twitter Business, accessed November 5, 2018, https://business.twitter.com/en/help/campaign-setup/campaign-targeting.html.

4. "What's in Your Home Timeline," Twitter Help, accessed November 5, 2018, https://help.twitter.com/en/using-twitter/twitter-timeline.

5. "Inactive Account Policy," Twitter Help, accessed November 9, 2018, https://help.twitter.com/en/rules-and-policies/inactive-twitter-accounts.

6. Noah Smith, "Twitter's Problem Isn't the Like Button," BNN Bloomberg, October 30, 2018, https://www.bnnbloomberg.ca/twitter-s-problem-isn-t-the-like-button-1.1160587.

CHAPTER 4: YOUTUBE

1. Dan Price, "The Fifteen Most-Watched YouTube Videos of All Time," Make Use Of, August 6, 2018, https://www.makeuseof.com/tag/most-watched-youtube-videos/.

2. Erica Smith and Monica Anderson, "Social Media Use in 2019," Pew Research Center Online, March 1, 2018, http://www.pewinternet.org/2018/03/01/social-media-use-in-2018/.

3. "YouTube Partner Program Overview," YouTube Help, accessed January 15, 2019, https://support.google.com/youtube/answer/72851.

4. Amy X. Wang, "YouTube Won't Allow 'Dangerous' Stunt Videos Anymore," *Rolling Stone*, January 17, 2019, https://www.rollingstone.com/music/music-news/youtube-birdbox-drake-challenge-780470/.

5. Leslie Walker, "How to Use YouTube," Lifewire, June 18, 2018, https://www.lifewire.com/how-to-use-youtube-2655498.

6. Shubhra Shalini, "Bird Box Challenge Leads YouTube to Strengthen Policy against Dangerous Videos," *International Business Times*, January 16, 2019, https://www.ibtimes.com/bird-box-challenge-leads-youtube-strengthen-policy-against-dangerous-videos-2752872.

CHAPTER 5: SNAPCHAT

1. Kit Smith, "123 Amazing Social Media Statistics and Facts," Brandwatch.com, March 1, 2019, https://www.brandwatch.com/blog/amazing-social-media-statistics-and-facts/.

2. Shona Ghosh, "6 Reasons Snapchat Is Losing Popularity," *Business Insider*, February 5, 2019, https://www.businessinsider.com/snapchat-losing-popularity-social-media-app-facebook-tiktok-2019-1.

3. Andrew Hutchinson, "Snapchat Launches Virtual Art Gallery for Black History Month," *SocialMediaToday*, February 12, 2019, https://www.socialmediatoday.com/news/snapchat-launches-virtual-art-gallery-for-black-history-month/548171/.

CHAPTER 6: INSTAGRAM

1. Dave Lawrence, "How to Use Instagram for Real Estates to Attract Your #Dream-Lead," *AdEspresso by Hootsuite* (blog), July 18, 2018, https://adespresso.com/blog/instagram-for-real-estates/.
2. Rachel Kraus, "Can an 'Instagram Museum' Have Phone-Free Moments? 29Rooms Gives It a Shot," Mashable, December 5, 2018, https://mashable.com/article/29rooms-phone-free-experiences/.
3. "The Best Wedding Hashtag Tips (and How to Make Your Own)," The Knot, accessed December 1, 2018, https://www.theknot.com/content/wedding-hashtag-tips.
4. "How Do I Delete My Account?" Instagram Help Center, accessed December 2, 2018, https://help.instagram.com.

CHAPTER 7: REDDIT

1. Will Nicol, "What Is Reddit? A Beginner's Guide to the Front Page of the Internet," Digital Trends, July 19, 2018, https://www.digitaltrends.com/social-media/what-is-reddit/.
2. Brett Molina, "Reddit Is Extremely Popular: Here's How to Watch What Your Kids Are Doing," *USA Today*, August 31, 2017, https://www.usatoday.com/story/tech/talkingtech/2017/08/31/reddit-extremely-popular-heres-how-watch-what-your-kids-doing/607996001/.
3. Molina, "Reddit Is Extremely Popular."
4. Melissa Suran and Danielle K. Kilgo, "Freedom from the Press? How Anonymous Gatekeepers on Reddit Covered the Boston Marathon Bombing," *Journalism Studies* 18, no. 8 (2015): 1035–51, doi: 10.1080/1461670X.2015.1111160.
5. Molina, "Reddit Is Extremely Popular."
6. Fernando Alfonso III, "Reddit Bans Infamous Forum about Beating Women," *Daily Dot*, June 10, 2014, https://www.dailydot.com/news/reddit-beating-women-banned/.
7. Nicol, "What Is Reddit?"
8. Guy Adams, "Internet's Biggest Troll Says Sorry . . . 'to Some Degree'; Blogger behind 'Jailbait' Forum Claims Reddit Staff 'Encouraged' Him," *Independent*, October 19, 2012, https://www.independent.co.uk/news/world/americas/internets-biggest-troll-says-sorry-to-some-degree-8218934.html.

CHAPTER 8: LINKEDIN

1. "About LinkedIn," LinkedIn, accessed January 1, 2019, https://about.linkedin.com/.

2. Katie Levinson, "How to Encourage Employees to Advocate for Your Brand on Social Media," *LinkedIn Marketing Solutions Blog*, October 26, 2017, https://busi ness.linkedin.com/marketing-solutions/blog/linkedin-elevate/2017/how-to-encourage -employees-to-advocate-for-your-brand-on-social-.

3. Kyungsun (Melissa) Rhee, Elina H. Hwang, and Yong Tan, "Social Hiring: The Right LinkedIn Connection That Helps You Land a Job," SSRN, October 5, 2018, http://dx.doi.org/10.2139/ssrn.3261180.

4. Marissa Boulanger, "Scraping the Bottom of the Barrel: Why It Is No Surprise That Data Scrapers Can Have Access to Public Profiles on LinkedIn," *SMU Science and Technology Law Review* 77 (2018), https://scholar.smu.edu/cgi/viewcontent.cgi?article =1275&context=scitech.

5. "User Agreement," LinkedIn, effective May 8, 2018, https://www.linkedin.com/ legal/user-agreement.

6. "Privately Looking for a Job," LinkedIn Help, accessed January 4, 2019, https:// www.linkedin.com/help/linkedin/answer/27/privately-looking-for-a-job?lang=en.

CHAPTER 9: TUMBLR

1. Daniel Nations, "What Is Microblogging?" Lifewire, November 12, 2018, https:// www.lifewire.com/what-is-microblogging-3486200.

2. "Sign up. Tumblr." Tumblr Registration Page, accessed February 11, 2019, https://www.tumblr.com/register/.

3. Jonah Engel Bromwich and Katie Van Syckle, "Tumblr Fans Abandon Ship as Tumblr Bans Porn," *New York Times*, December 8, 2018, https://www.nytimes .com/2018/12/06/style/tumblr-porn.html.

4. "Tumblr Labs." Tumblr, accessed February 20, 2019, https://www.tumblr.com /settings/labs.

5. "Tumblr Labs," Tumblr Settings, Labs, accessed February 2, 2019, https://www .tumblr.com/settings/labs.

CHAPTER 10: PINTEREST

1. "Terms of Service," Pinterest, accessed January 1, 2019, https://policy.pinterest .com/en/terms-of-service.

2. Elise Moreau, "What Is Pinterest? An Intro to Using the Social Image Platform," Lifewire, September 10, 2018, https://www.lifewire.com/how-to-use-pinterest -3486578.

3. "How to Use Pinterest to Plan Your Wedding," *The Garter Girl Blog*, accessed January 1, 2019, https://thegartergirl.com/blogs/the-garter-girls-blog/how-to-use-pin terest-to-plan-your-wedding.

4. "Terms of Service," Pinterest, accessed January 1, 2019, https://policy.pinterest .com/en/terms-of-service.

5. "Save Pins with the Pinterest Browser Button," Pinterest Help Center, accessed January 2, 2019, https://help.pinterest.com/en/article/save-pins-with-the-pinterest -browser-button.

CHAPTER 11: OTHER NOTABLE SOCIAL MEDIA PLATFORMS

1. "How to Verify Your Address," Nextdoor Help, accessed March 25, 2019, https://help.nextdoor.com/s/article/How-to-verify-your-address?language=en_US.

2. "How the Internet Has Changed Dating," *Economist*, August 18, 2018, https:// www.economist.com/briefing/2018/08/18/how-the-internet-has-changed-dating.

3. "Ancestry Support," Ancestry.com, accessed March 20, 2019, https://support .ancestry.com/s/.

4. "Downloading AncestryDNA Raw Data," Ancestry.com, accessed March 20, 2019, https://support.ancestry.com/s/article/Downloading-Raw-DNA-Data -1460089696533; "Accessing and Downloading Your Raw Data," 23andMe.com, accessed March 20, 2019, https://customercare.23andme.com/hc/en-us/articles/ 212196868-Accessing-and-Downloading-Your-Raw-Data.

5. "Best Secure Mobile Messaging Apps," TechWorld, January 4, 2019, https:// www.techworld.com/security/best-secure-mobile-messaging-apps-3629914/.

6. Lily Hay Newman, "Encrypted Messaging Isn't Magic," *Wired*, June 14, 2018, https://www.wired.com/story/encrypted-messaging-isnt-magic/.

7. Mark Williams, "Secure Messaging Apps Comparison," accessed March 9, 2019, https://www.securemessagingapps.com/.

8. Newman, "Encrypted Messaging Isn't Magic."

9. "Frequently Asked Questions," 4Chan, accessed March 10, 2019, http:// www.4chan.org/faq.

CHAPTER 12: ARCHIVING, SAVING, AND LEGACY MANAGEMENT

1. "Looking Ahead," Flickr, accessed April 10, 2019, https://www.flickr.com/look ingahead/.

2. "What Is Digi.me?" Digi.me, accessed April 1, 2019, https://digi.me/what-is -digime/.

3. "Get a Copy of What You've Shared on Instagram," Instagram Settings, accessed March 3, 2019, https://www.instagram.com/download/request/.

4. "redditPostArchiver," GitHub, accessed March 3, 2019, https://github.com/pl77/redditPostArchiver.

INDEX

ABOUT THE AUTHOR

Melody Karle is a librarian at the University of Houston Libraries, where she manages data organization and records management projects. She writes about social media, personal digital archiving, digital file management, personal information management, the internet of things, personal technology, and libraries. At home, she is a gardener and animal rescue volunteer. Her previous book, *Managing the Digital You*, was released in paperback in early 2019.